66 BOOKS:
ONE STORY

How the whole Bible points to Jesus

66 BOOKS: ONE STORY

How the whole Bible points to Jesus

Paul Reynolds

10 9 8 7 6 5 4 3 2
Copyright © 2023 Paul Reynolds
ISBN: 978-1-5271-0894-3
First published in 2013.
This edition published in 2023
by Christian Focus Publications,
Geanies House, Fearn, Tain, Ross-shire, IV20 1TW, U.K.
Illustrations, Cover and chapter page design by Sarah Douglas
Printed in China

DEDICATION
For Jude and Alice

Paul Reynolds has written an excellent resource for children, parents and churches. This book navigates the 66 books of the Bible, leading always to the Savior. If you use this book, your children will hear the gospel to the praise and glory of God and our Savior Jesus Christ.

John and Keri Folmar
United Christian Church of Dubai in the United Arab Emirates

66 Books, 1 Story is an excellent teaching and reference resource for elementary children's ministry, Sunday School, or home schooling. Each chapter provides a basic introduction and overview of each Bible book as well as key teaching points. The "Salvation Thread" section, relates the message of the book to the over-arching message of the Bible. I'm thankful for such a well-written resources that will provide an excellent supplement both for teaching and family devotions.

Jared Kennedy
Editor, The Gospel Coalition

It is so exciting to see God's beautiful tale of redemption through stories of the Bible unfolded in a format such as 66BoS. The questions, references, thread, and overview all point to knowing God as our rescuer and hero. I look forward with anticipation to using this devotion with my children, young adult Bible studies, and as a gift to others seeking to know the truth. *66 Books One Story* is a wonderful tool to see the consistency of who God was, is, and always will be.

Joani Burchett
Mother of five boys aged 5-15

Ever wonder how so many different books belong to the same volume, the Bible? Here is a most lively, memorable, and engaging expedition through every book of Holy Scripture. While the different authors, characters and modes are recognized and explored, everything in them centers on the one fundamental truth: the gospel of Jesus Christ. This guide makes the entire Bible really accessible.

William Edgar
Professor of Apologetics, Westminster Theological Seminary, Philadelphia, U.S.A.

66 Books One Story is a wonderful resource for families. In just over two months, your children can have a deeper understanding of each book of the Bible, and of Scripture as a whole. Most importantly, they would walk away with a new appreciation for who God is and what his plan for us entails.

Danika Cooley
Blogger, curriculum developer, and writer at ThinkingKidsBlog.org
Author of the Who What Why series, and *Wonderfully Made*

CONTENTS

ACKNOWLEDGEMENTS

There are three people to whom I am in ever-increasing debt, and they are the first I should thank.

My wife, Rachael, has been my best friend since I was sixteen and the love of my life since I was eighteen. She is my first and primary go-to person for encouragement, advice, perspective, insight, fresh thinking and a dose of sanity.

My parents Timothy and Marjolein Reynolds are the most faithful servants of the Most High God whom I have ever met, and they have been making deposits of prayer and Scripture into my life since before I was born. It is because of them that an idea like this book would even occur to me, and in God's grace it is down to them that I have any grasp of the majestic, all-encompassing and glorious nature of God's Word.

They were joined by a number of others in giving time, energy, thought and feedback to my various drafts and ideas. First, my brother David with his relentless editor's eye, then Joani Burchett who was a great encouragement through the four years it took to complete this project. The fine-tuning of Renee Howell and Ruth Haynes was also gratefully received.

The blessings of a focused and godly boss are not to be underestimated, particularly when you can count that man as your pastor and close friend. Thabiti Anyabwile was all those things for me as I wrote.

Many other friends provided support and encouragement along the way, particularly my brothers and sisters at First Baptist Church of Grand Cayman with whom I live and worship. Thank you.

Finally, Catherine Mackenzie of Christian Focus has my respect and gratitude for taking me on as a first-time author. She showed great patience with me in bringing this project to life, and I pray that God will continue to bless her work and life.

Now to Him, who has already done more than all I could ever ask or imagine, "to the only God my Savior, be glory, majesty, power and authority, through Jesus Christ our Lord, before all ages, now and for evermore! Amen" (Jude 25).

Paul Reynolds

INTRODUCTION

But as for you, continue in what you have learned and have become convinced of, because you know those from whom you learned it, and how from infancy you have known the holy Scriptures, which are able to make you wise for salvation through faith in Christ Jesus. All Scripture is God-breathed and is useful for teaching, rebuking, correcting and training in righteousness, so that the man of God may be thoroughly equipped for every good work.

2 Timothy 3:14-16

Some parts of the Bible – particularly the narrative sections – lend themselves more easily to teaching children. And yet the *entire* Bible is God's gift to our children, just as much as to parents and other adults. That's the joy and challenge of sharing the Word with our children: helping them see it's for them. God inspired all of it to be for all of us, as he reveals different parts of Himself in different ways in different parts of his Word.

Underpinning this is the idea that the Bible is not primarily a library or collection, but one story: the story of how God created the world and has been preparing a people and a creation for himself through the work of his Son Jesus Christ. That story has taken many twists and turns and involves law, prophecy, poetry and letters. Jesus said so himself to the two men on the road to Emmaus in Luke 24:27: "… *beginning with Moses and all the Prophets, he explained to them what was said in all the Scriptures concerning himself.*"

Often, children have so little contact with the non-narrative sections of the Bible that they miss much of what God is saying. When they are old enough to read the Bible for themselves, it is then natural for them to ignore those large chunks of Scripture they are not used to. In doing so they miss much of what God tells us about sin, and do not see God's relentless grace and compassion painted in broad and fine strokes across the vast canvas of Old Testament prophecy.

The reason for this book is therefore to introduce people to every book in the Bible, and is aimed primarily at ages seven through twelve. As parents, when we teach our children from the Bible it exposes our lack of knowledge and understanding. My hope therefore is to also provide parents with a useful overview of Scripture to use as a base not just for teaching their children but also for their own study.

THE FORMAT

This book can be used either by parents with younger children, or by older children on their own. For the older children, it would be helpful for them to have a notebook and pen handy to write down their answers to the various questions at the end of each chapter. It can be used as a devotion with each chapter perhaps spread over multiple days depending on the time available.

Each chapter *66 Books One Story* covers a book of the Bible, with the exceptions of Genesis and Psalms, where I use two chapters for each book; and 2 and 3 John, which I have dealt with in a single chapter.

Each chapter has a number of parts:

Sub-heading: A single-phrased motto or summary of the Bible book.

Introduction: What is of particular interest in this book? Who wrote it? When?

Overview: The book itself retold in approximately 350 words or less. Next to the summary are paragraph numbers referenced in the 'Learning from' section to show you where to find each learning point.

Most of the overview consists of paraphrased/condensed quotations from the Bible. Where I have directly quoted from the Bible, it is printed in red.

Learning From: How does the book apply to us today? Cross-references are included to pinpoint where the Bible teaches us these things. Some of the questions are designed to provoke discussion, others to reinforce truths, others to help understand where the child's heart is. This means there are some open and some closed questions.

Salvation Thread: An overview of how the whole book, or an example of how part of the book fits into God's story of salvation.

Key verse: A verse useful for memorization.

KEY WORD GLOSSARY

One challenge with trying to bring the language of a reliable and accurate retelling of Scripture to children is vocabulary. The temptation is to remove all words that children will not already be familiar with through school and friends, but this involves reducing or obscuring the meaning of some fundamental biblical concepts.

Where possible therefore I have tried to keep the vocabulary unchallenging in order to smooth the way to understanding, but have also chosen to retain a number of key biblical words. For example, 'repent'. Alternative and more child-friendly words miss the aspects of turning away from our sinful attitudes towards God and wanting to love him through obedience.

To help with understanding these words I have included a 'Key Word Glossary' at the back, including examples from Scripture of where they are used.

I pray that God will use this book in opening up his Word so that more and more children will know from their hearts that "*all Scripture is God-breathed and is useful …*" (2 Timothy 3:16).

LAW

The book of
GENESIS

GENESIS 1–11

Creation to Babel: History begins, sin starts and a Savior is promised

INTRODUCTION

- God made a perfect universe from nothing. But people spoiled it because they thought they knew better than God, and disobeyed him. But, God didn't stop loving people. Moses wrote the book of Genesis (which means, 'beginning'), shortly before the *Israelites* entered the *promised land* after escaping from Egypt.

- Genesis was probably written some time between 1446 and 1406 B.C.

OVERVIEW

1. "In the beginning, God made everything: day and night; sea and sky; land, plants and trees; sun, moon and stars; fish, birds and animals. Finally he made Adam and Eve to live in a wonderful place called the Garden of Eden. God saw that everything he had made was very good, and then he rested."

2. "God said to Adam and Eve that they could eat from any tree except one, but *Satan*, in the form of a snake, said if they ate that one fruit they would be like God."

3. "Being like God sounded good, and the fruit looked tasty, so Eve ate it and then Adam."

4. "Because Adam and Eve did not obey God he had to send them away from the Garden. They could not now live forever. Disobeying God meant they would have pain and one day die. *Satan* would hurt people, but God promised that one day a man would be born who would beat *Satan*."

5. "Many years later when there were lots of people, God saw that everyone wanted to do bad things all the time. This made God sad because he hates *sin*. He decided to start again with one man, Noah, and his family, who still loved God and were trying to obey him."

6. "He told Noah to build a huge boat called an ark, for himself and his family. Also for two of most kinds of animal and seven of some animals. When God flooded the earth all of the other animals and people died. Afterwards, God used a rainbow as a symbol to promise he would never do that again."

7. "Much later, lots of people got together and tried to build a city that would make them look great. They thought they had a better plan than God and didn't want to spread over the earth as he told them to. To stop them, God made everyone speak different languages. Then they had to go to different places."

LEARNING FROM GENESIS 1-11

1. God made everything perfect. It is only because of *sin* that there is anything bad in the world (See overview paragraphs 1–2).

   Bible references: Genesis 3:15-19; Haggai 1:9-10; Romans 5:12.

   Questions: What are some of the lovely things that God has made? What are some of the bad things that are in the world because of *sin*?

2. God hates *sin* and will not put up with it forever (See overview paragraphs 4–6).

   Bible references: Genesis 6:5-7; Proverbs 6:16-19; 2 Thessalonians 1:8-9.

   Questions: What bad things do you want to do? How do you feel about them? Do you sometimes try to do things your way instead of God's way?

3. God defeated the *devil* – as he promised – through Jesus dying on the cross and coming to life again. The devil still hurts people, but because of what Jesus has done we can have our sins forgiven and not be punished (See overview paragraph 4).

   Bible references: Genesis 3:15; 1 John 3:8.

   Question: Have you asked God to forgive your *sin*?

SALVATION THREAD

"And I will put enmity between you and the woman, and between your offspring and hers; he will crush your head, and you will strike his heel" (Genesis 3:15).

This is the first time in the Bible that God talks about Jesus coming. *Satan* hates all people and wants to mess up God's work, including Jesus' mission to save us. He thought he had won when evil men killed Jesus, but Jesus had the victory because he rose from the dead. Genesis gives us the bad news about *sin* and death, but it also gives us the good news of God making a way for people to be saved.

"For just as through the disobedience of the one man the many were made sinners, so also through the obedience of the one man the many will be made righteous" (Romans 5:19).

The *apostle* Paul compared Adam (the disobedient man) with Jesus (the perfectly obedient man). Adam's sin means that all have sinned. Jesus' obedience, which included his death, means that many people are saved.

Key Verse: "In the beginning God created the heavens and the earth … God saw all that he had made, and it was very good" (Genesis 1:1, 31a).

GENESIS 12-50

Abraham to Joseph: God separates a group of people for himself

INTRODUCTION

- Burning cities, lies, family break–ups, kidnap, prison and famine. All this and more was in the lives of four men chosen by God to do his work: Abraham, Abraham's son Isaac, Isaac's son Jacob, and Jacob's son Joseph. The second half of Genesis tells the story of God separating a group of people for himself; not because they were great, but just because he decided to love them in a special way.

- Genesis was probably written some time between 1446 and 1406 B.C.

OVERVIEW

1. "God told Abram to go to a new country (but didn't tell him at first where it would be). God said that he would do great things for Abram, and that through him people all over the world would be blessed. Abram obeyed God."

2. "God changed Abram's name to Abraham, which means 'father of many people'. God said that Abraham would have more children than the stars in the sky, and that Abraham, his children, and their children would be given the whole country that he was living in. Abraham believed and trusted God, and God made him righteous and gave him the free gift of forgiveness. Abraham was not perfect and did some bad things, but God kept his promise that he would have children. He and his wife had a son even though they were very old, and they called him Isaac."

3. "Later, God told Abraham to *sacrifice* Isaac and Abraham trusted God enough to obey. Just as Abraham was about to kill him for the sacrifice God said, 'No – don't kill the boy.' God provided a goat for the *sacrifice* instead. When Isaac grew up he had two sons, called Jacob and Esau. Jacob tricked Esau to get good things from their Dad and from God. Even though Jacob acted badly, God had chosen to bless him."

4. "One of Jacob's sons was called Joseph. Joseph's ten older brothers were jealous of him because their Dad loved him most. They sold him to some people for money, and he became a slave in Egypt, and later he was put in prison for something he didn't do."

5. "God was with Joseph and showed him the meaning of some dreams of Pharaoh(the ruler of Egypt), that no-one else could explain. Pharaoh thought Joseph was such a good man that he put him in charge of everything. Joseph made sure there was food for everyone, even in years when there was no rain to make the crops grow."

6. "Joseph's brothers and his father, Jacob, then went to live with him in Egypt. Their family came to be very, very big."

LEARNING FROM GENESIS 12-50

1. Abraham obeyed God because he trusted him. He knew that God always keeps his promises (See overview paragraphs 1–2).

   Bible references: Genesis 12:1, 4; 15:6; Romans 4:1-5; 1 John 1:9.

   Questions: Do you trust God's promises, such as the promise that God forgives the sins of all those who repent?

2. God is in charge. He can use anyone for important work – even people like Abraham and Jacob who did bad things. And he will save anyone from their sins, whatever they have done before. So ask God for forgiveness, and serve God today – don't worry about how good you think you are. (See overview paragraphs 3–4).

   Bible references: Genesis 28:13-15; Malachi 1:2-3; Luke 15:7.

   Questions: Do you realize that God can forgive your sins, no matter how bad you are? And that when he has done that, you can do wonderful things for God?

3. God is in control of everything. Even when things seem to be going badly we can trust him that he is doing good things (See overview paragraphs 4–6).

   Bible references: Genesis 50:20; Romans 8:28; Philippians 1:12-14.

   Question: Where else in the Bible have bad things happened that God has used for good?[1]

SALVATION THREAD

"And I will put enmity between you and the woman, and between your offspring and hers; he will crush your head, and you will strike his heel" (Genesis 3:15).

This is the first time in the Bible that God talks about Jesus coming. Satan hates all people and wants to mess up God's work, including Jesus' mission to save us. He thought he had won when evil men killed Jesus, but Jesus had the victory because he rose from the dead. Genesis gives us the bad news about sin and death, but it also gives us the good news of God making a way for people to be saved.

"For just as through the disobedience of the one man the many were made sinners, so also through the obedience of the one man the many will be made righteous" (Romans 5:19).

The apostle Paul compares Adam (the disobedient man) with Jesus (the perfectly obedient man). Adam's sin means that all have sinned. Jesus' obedience, which includes his death, means that many people are saved.

Key Verse: "In the beginning God created the heavens and the earth … God saw all that he had made, and it was very good" (Genesis 1:1, 31a).

---

1. For example: Paul in prison (Philippians 1:12-14); Jesus was killed, which helped bring salvation; Esther was forced to marry a wicked king, and she could help save the Israelites because of it. Christians in Jerusalem were persecuted, so they ran away and told people in many more places about the gospel of Jesus (Acts 8:1, 4).

The book of
EXODUS

EXODUS

God rescues his people from slavery

INTRODUCTION

- This book focuses on a murderer who ran away (Moses), and a leader who took a million people on an escape from slavery (also Moses!). It tells about how God rescued his people from their terrible life in Egypt. The book of Exodus was written by Moses and includes the history of the Israelites from when Moses was born, until they were in the desert waiting to go into the *promised land*.

- The exodus from Egypt may have happened in 1446 B.C.

OVERVIEW

1. "After Jacob's whole family of seventy joined Joseph to live in Egypt, the family grew over many years. They were known as the *Israelites*. Eventually, there were so many of them that the Egyptians were afraid they might take over the country. To stop that happening, they made the Israelites slaves. They even tried to kill all the baby boys, but baby Moses was kept safe."

2. "When Moses had grown up, God told him that he would lead the *Israelites* out of Egypt. However, Pharaoh wouldn't let God's people go, even though God sent ten plagues to Egypt so that Pharaoh and the *Israelites* would know God is real. Only after the last plague did Pharaoh give in, but then he changed his mind and went with his whole army to chase them and bring them back. When the Israelites got to the Red Sea, God made a path through the sea so they could walk across. When the Egyptian army tried to get across after them, God let the sea go back so they were all drowned."

3. "God told his people to have a special celebration every year to remember how God saves his people and punishes those who say no to God."

4. "Later the *Israelites* started complaining because they had no food, so God made it rain bread and gave them meat so they would have enough to eat."

5. "When they reached Mount Sinai, God gave Moses the *Ten Commandments*, and lots of other laws to make sure the people treated each other in the right way and looked after those in need. God also told Moses exactly how to build a tabernacle, which was a special place to bring sacrifices and worship God."

6. "But Moses was up the mountain a long time hearing from God, and the people were tired of waiting for him to come back down. They asked Aaron to make them an idol –

a golden calf – to worship that instead of God. This was evil and made God very angry, but Moses begged and God promised to stay with them."

7. "Much later, lots of people got together and tried to build a city that would make them look great. They thought they had a better plan than God and didn't want to spread over the earth as he told them to. So, God made everyone speak different languages. Then they had to go to different places."

LEARNING FROM EXODUS

1. God rescues his people. He did some amazing things to free the Israelites from slavery and he has done an even more amazing thing to free his people from the slavery of sin (See overview paragraphs 2 and 4).

    Bible references: Exodus 3:7-8, 14:21-23; Romans 6:6; Hebrews 9:15.

    Questions: What amazing things did God do for the *Israelites*? What amazing thing did God do so that his people can be freed from *sin*?

2. We easily forget that God is real, and all that God does for us. Even the *Israelites*, who had seen God do amazing miracles, forgot him and worshiped an idol (See overview paragraphs 3 and 5).

    Bible references: Exodus 13:3; Deuteronomy 6:12; 2 Timothy 2:8.

    Questions: What has God done that you should remember? What did God tell the *Israelites* to do that would help them to remember? What can you do and where can you go to help you to remember?

3. God shows us that he is real, caring and powerful. The *Israelites* needed to remember it so they would trust him to rescue them from Egypt. We need to remember it so we can trust him to forgive our sins if we ask him (See overview paragraph 2).

    Bible references: Exodus 6:7, 7:5; Psalm 46:10; John 17:3.

    Questions: Why did God send the plagues on Egypt? How important is it that God is real?

SALVATION THREAD

"For we know that our old self was *crucified* with [Jesus] so that the body of *sin* might be done away with, that we should no longer be slaves to *sin* …" (Romans 6:6).

God's people were made slaves in Egypt, and the Bible talks about all of us being slaves to *sin* unless God saves us. In Exodus we see how God performed amazing miracles to save his people from slavery in Egypt. He took them into the *promised land* and said if they were obedient to him, he would always be with them.

Jesus' birth, life, death and rising from the dead is one amazing miracle. God did it so his people would not have to be slaves to sin any more. Instead of punishment, they become his children, free to make God happy with a new life of loving and obeying him.

Key Verse: "I am the Lord, and I will bring you out from under the yoke of the Egyptians. I will free you from being slaves to them, and I will redeem you with an outstretched arm and with mighty acts of judgment. I will take you as my own people, and I will be your God" (Exodus 6:6).

The book of
LEVITICUS

LEVITICUS

A people set apart for God

INTRODUCTION

- Sacrifices, offerings, skin diseases and rules. Doesn't sound exciting, does it? But with a million people living together in the desert, some of God's new laws saved them from being wiped out by disease, while other laws helped them to love and worship God. During the year that the *Israelites* were camped by Mount Sinai, Moses received the *Ten Commandments* from God. God gave the other instructions to Moses when he came back down.

- Leviticus was probably written some time between 1446 and 1406 B.C.

OVERVIEW

1. "The LORD spoke to Moses from the Tabernacle."

2. "The people need to make offerings to me," he said. "These offerings remind you to ask me to forgive you, and to thank me for everything I do for you. Some of these offerings will mean killing a perfect animal, and for some of them I will send fire from heaven to burn the offering. These things show that sin has been paid for and that you are forgiven."

3. "Moses' brother Aaron and his sons were made priests for God. They were in charge of making the offerings to God and looking after the Tabernacle. However, Aaron's two sons disobeyed God, so God killed them to show how serious sin is and how holy God is."

4. "God told Moses about other rules that the *Israelites* had to follow. Many rules were about keeping things clean so that people did not get sick. Others were about what they must not do. When God gave all the rules he said, '*Be holy because I, the* LORD *your God, am holy.*' God also said what some of the punishments had to be. For some sins a person would be sent away from God's people or even put to death. One man said bad things about God and he had to be put to death."

5. "There were also special times for God's people to celebrate who God is and everything he had done for them."

6. "God said to his people, 'I will always be with you if you obey what I tell you. But if you do not obey me then I will not be with you, and that would be horrible for you.'"

LEARNING FROM LEVITICUS

1. It is very important to understand how serious *sin* is. Then we can understand why we need to get rid of it from our lives (See overview paragraphs 2–4).

   Bible references: Leviticus 18:24-25; Deuteronomy 9:4; Romans 6:2, 23.

   Questions: What did God tell the *Israelites* to do that showed how serious sin is?

2. God is holy. This means that he has no *sin* in him – he never thinks, says or does anything wrong, and always does and says what is right. He wants us to be *holy* like him (See overview paragraph 4).

   Bible references: Leviticus 11:44-45; Psalm 99:8-9; 1 Peter 1:15-16.

   Question: Do you think there are any sins that God doesn't really care about? Where can we find out about God's rules for our lives?

3. God loves to forgive his people for their sins and to do other good things for them. We should thank and praise him for all these things (See overview paragraphs 3, 5, and 6).

   Bible references: Leviticus 6:6-7; Deuteronomy 26:11; Luke 1:53-55.

   Question: Make a list of all the wonderful things that God has done for you. (Remember: everything that is good comes from God!) What is the best thing that God can do for you?

SALVATION THREAD

The book of Leviticus helps us to understand why Jesus had to die. Our sins have to be forgiven and Leviticus shows us how serious *sin* is. Some people think that *sin* just means being a little less than perfect, or just being normal. Leviticus shows us that *sin* is really an act of rebellion against God and it deserves death.

Some of the offerings in Leviticus involved killing an animal, which reminded people that *sin* leads to death, but it also pointed to the ultimate *sacrifice* – Jesus. Because of his death, the sins of all God's people are forgiven – that's why we don't need to do animal sacrifices any more. The sacrifices pointed to Jesus, and he has already come, and died … and risen to life again! (See Hebrews 10:3-4, 10).

Key Verse: "I am the LORD who brought you up out of Egypt to be your God; therefore be *holy*, because I am *holy*" (Leviticus 11:45).

The book of
NUMBERS

NUMBERS

'In the desert'[2]

INTRODUCTION

- They were so close. But after walking from Egypt to the border of the *promised land* in just a few months, the *Israelites* couldn't get in for forty years because of their disobedience and grumbling. Numbers was written by Moses, and starts at the time when the *Israelites* were by Mount Sinai, where God gave them the *Ten Commandments*. It finishes when they are still in the desert nearly forty years later, about to go into the *promised land*.

- Numbers was probably written some time between 1446 and 1406 B.C.

OVERVIEW

1. "God told Moses to make a list of all the men in Israel old enough to be in the army – there were over six hundred thousand[3]. Moses didn't count the tribe of Levi, because they would not be soldiers – their job was looking after the Tabernacle, helping the people to worship God. Moses went to the Tent of Meeting, where he spoke to God and God spoke to him. God reminded Moses that the *Israelites* must celebrate the Passover every year to remember how he had saved them and punished the Egyptians. God covered the Tent of Meeting with a pillar of cloud all day, and a cloud of fire all night. When he moved the cloud, it was the sign that it was time for the people to move."

2. "God then told Moses to send out leaders to explore the land of Canaan – the *promised land* God was going to give them. They came back and said the country was full of good food but the people and cities were too big and strong to attack. This made the *Israelites* complain to Moses again, and they wanted to get rid of him. Moses' sister and brother and a group of leaders all spoke against Moses."

3. "Speaking against Moses was speaking against God, because God had chosen Moses. "'*How long will they refuse to believe in me …*' said God, '*even though I have done so many miracles in front of them?*'[4] God was angry but Moses asked him to keep on forgiving the people for their sins. God said yes, but those who had not trusted him would not be allowed to go into the *promised land*. Later the people complained again, about not having enough water. God again sent punishment, and again the people were sorry."

4. "When the *Israelites* moved closer to the *promised land* they were attacked four times by different armies. God gave the Israelites victory every time, but they still didn't obey God. Many started to worship a false god. Again God had to punish them to show them their sin, and many died."

---

2. 'In the desert' was the original name of the book, before it was changed to 'Numbers', many years later, by Bible translators.
3. About the same population size as modern-day Charlotte in the US, and Glasgow in the U.K.
4. Numbers 14:11.

5. "Then God gave Moses more instructions for the people, and showed him the *promised land* from the top of a mountain."

LEARNING FROM NUMBERS

1. God always keeps his promises to us, even though we don't keep our promises to him. The Israelites promised to obey God and they soon disobeyed him again. They thanked him and then soon grumbled again. They repented of worshiping false gods and then did it again. But God still took them into the *promised land*, just like he said he would (See overview paragraphs 1–4).

   Bible references: Numbers 14:19-20; Joshua 21:45; Romans 5:8.

   Questions: What promise to the *Israelites* did God keep, even though the Israelites broke theirs? Can you think of promises that you have made, or people have made to you, that have been broken? How does knowing that God always keeps his promises affect how you think about him? Do you trust him?

2. Grumbling and complaining is disobedience to God and He punished the Israelites for it, sometimes severely. This reminds us that sin is serious – God hates it and we also should hate sin (See overview paragraphs 2–4).

   Bible references: Numbers 14:17-23; Proverbs 3:7; 1 Corinthians 10:10-12.

   Questions: What are you tempted to grumble about? Try to remember all the ways God has blessed you, and you will feel less like complaining!

3. We can learn to trust God more, even when we're scared or sad, by remembering what he has done, by remembering that he keeps his promises. The *Israelites* forgot to trust God when they became scared thinking that he couldn't or wouldn't help them (See overview paragraph 3).

   Bible references: Numbers 14:11-12; Psalm 103:2, 7; Philippians 4:6.

   Questions: What things make you scared or sad? Now remember some of the things that God has given you or done for you. If God has done those things, is there any reason for us to be afraid?

SALVATION THREAD

The *apostle* Paul said that what happened to the Israelites in the desert is a warning to all of us to love God instead of loving evil.

The story also reminds us that "God is faithful; he will not let you be tempted beyond what you can bear. But when you are tempted, he will also provide a way out so that you can stand up under it" (Paul the apostle, in 1 Corinthians 10:13).

The God of 3,500 years ago in the desert is the same as the God of 2,000 years ago when Paul wrote to the Corinthians. And he is the same God now. He is faithful and patient, loving and *holy* – punishing sin and helping his people to obey him.

Key Verse: "Now may the LORD's strength be displayed, just as you have declared: 'The LORD is slow to anger, abounding in love and forgiving *sin* and rebellion. Yet he does not leave the guilty unpunished …'" (Numbers 14:17-18a).

The book of
DEUTERONOMY

DEUTERONOMY

'These are the words'[5]

INTRODUCTION

- Deuteronomy is Moses' last words to the *Israelites* before they went into the *promised land* and he went to heaven. He wanted them to remember what God had done for them and what God had told them to do, because he knew that "they are not just idle words for you – they are your life" (Deuteronomy 32:47).

- Deuteronomy was probably written some time between 1446 and 1406 B.C.

OVERVIEW

1. "Forty years after leaving Egypt, Moses gave the Israelites this message from God: '*Go and take possession of the land that I promised to give your fathers, to Abraham, Isaac and Jacob and all who came after them.*'"[6]

2. "'Hear the laws from God that I will teach you,' Moses said. 'Do not add to them and do not take anything away from them. Remember what God has done for you and teach it to your children and grandchildren. Worship only God – he is the only true God. *Love the LORD your God with all your heart and with all your soul and with all your strength.*'"[7]

3. "Moses continued, 'God loves you and has chosen you to be his special people. It's not because he thinks you are better than other people – he just loves you, that's it. Remember what he has done for you, remember that nothing can stop you when God is with you. Don't forget him like you did when you made the golden calf, or you will be destroyed.'"

4. "'Worship God in the way he tells you, not in the way that the wicked nations worship their false gods. Look after the poor (remember: you used to be slaves, so treating poor people well should be natural for you). Give God a tenth of all you have, celebrate the festivals God has given you to help you remember him, and treat people fairly. You have now become the people of the LORD your God.[8] If you obey the LORD he will bless you greatly, but if you disobey him terrible things will happen to you.'"

5. "Moses brought all the Israelites together and reminded them that God was there with them; they were making a covenant with him, promising to obey him. '*Blessed are you, O Israel!*' Moses said, '*Who is like you, a people saved by the LORD?*'"[9]

---

5. 'These are the words' is the translation of the original name of the book. The name 'Deuteronomy', meaning 'repeat of the law', comes from a mistake in the Latin translation. But that's still a good name for the book, so the name stayed.
6. Deuteronomy 1:8.
7. Deuteronomy 6:5.
8. Deuteronomy 27:9.
9. Deuteronomy 33:29.

6. "God showed Moses the *promised land* from up a mountain, and then Moses died. Since then, *no one has ever shown the mighty power or performed the awesome deeds that Moses did in the sight of all Israel.*[10] God knew Moses face to face."

LEARNING FROM DEUTERONOMY

1. God's love for his people has nothing to do with how good they are. God loves his people even though they are not especially good (See overview paragraph 3).

    Bible references: Deuteronomy 7:7; Hosea 3:1; 1 Corinthians 1:26-27.
    Questions: Parents love their children even when they are disobedient. How does that remind us of God's love?

2. Remembering who God is and what he has done for us should remind us that he is real and that he is God (See overview paragraphs 2–3).

    Bible references: Deuteronomy 4:34-35; Psalm 63:5-6; John 14:15.
    Questions: What had God done for the *Israelites* by this point in the story? What has God done for you? Who do you think that God is?

3. God's laws are perfect. The laws he gave to the Israelites were perfect, and the commands he gives to us are perfect. We should obey them, and not change them. (See overview paragraphs 2, 4–5).

    Bible references: Deuteronomy 8:1; Psalm 19:7; 1 John 3:23-24.
    Question: Can you think of any of God's commands to you that you don't want to obey? Why don't you want to obey them?

SALVATION THREAD

"I will raise up for them a *prophet* like you from among their brothers; I will put my words in his mouth, and he will tell them everything I command him. If anyone does not listen to my words that the *prophet* speaks in my name, I myself will call him to account" (Deuteronomy 18:18-19).

God gave that *prophecy* through Moses. He said a *prophet* would come and speak God's words to God's people – words of life that *needed to* be obeyed. When the special *prophet* came, he obeyed God perfectly, and his words were perfectly from God, and we must obey him in order to know the Father. That man said this: "For I did not speak of my own accord, but the Father who sent me commanded me what to say and how to say it. I know that his command leads to eternal life. So whatever I say is just what the Father has told me to say" (John 12:49-50).

That man is our Savior, Jesus Christ.

Key Verse: "... it was because the LORD loved you and kept the oath he swore to your forefathers that he brought you out with a mighty hand and redeemed you from the land of slavery, from the power of Pharaoh king of Egypt. Know therefore that the LORD your God is God; he is the faithful God ..." (Deuteronomy 7:8-9a).

---

10. Deuteronomy 34:12.

HISTORY

The book of
JOSHUA

JOSHUA

Home at last!

INTRODUCTION

- At last God's people arrived in the *promised land*, after 400 years in Egypt and forty years in the wilderness. As the story starts, they have a huge river to cross and lots of challenges before it can become their country. The book of Joshua covers the time between the death of Moses and the *tribes of Israel* settling in Canaan. We are not sure who wrote this book. Joshua probably wrote some of it and others might have finished it up to 300 years later.

- Joshua probably lived some time between about 1550 and 1440 B.C.

OVERVIEW

1. "After Moses died, God told Joshua, the new leader of Israel, that it was time to go into the *promised land* of Canaan, but a big river was in their way and there was no bridge. God briefly stopped the River Jordan from flowing, so all the water piled up on one side. Everyone walked across on the dried up river, thanks to God's miracle. All the men were then circumcised and the people celebrated God taking them out of Egypt."

2. "Soon they came to the first city they had to attack, called Jericho. It seemed too well-defended for the *Israelites* to attack, because a huge wall went all the way around the city to protect it. However, God made that wall fall down so the Israelites could win the battle. God told Israel that everyone in the city must be killed and they couldn't keep anything they found in the city, which used to belong to the people there."

3. "However, a man called Achan kept some things for himself so God was angry and Israel's enemies won the next battle. Achan had to be put to death because he had gone against God's instructions; after that, God again gave his people victory in battle."

4. "Joshua read to the people all the Words of God that Moses had written, and made offerings to God. After that, Israel won a lot of battles in the *promised land* and defeated thirty-one kings, although they didn't manage to take over the whole country. After seven years of battles God gave them a time of peace and rest. They divided up the land fairly between the twelve tribes of Israel."

5. "Before Joshua died he reminded the people how important it was to obey God. The people of Canaan who were left didn't believe in God and ignored him; the *Israelites* must avoid them otherwise they would be tempted to ignore God as well. God had done wonderful things for his people and they should always serve him. The people agreed when Joshua said all these things."

LEARNING FROM JOSHUA

1. God kept his promise and took his people into the *promised land*. The most wonderful promise that God has kept for his people is to save them from their sins through Jesus. One way to know we can trust God to keep his promises is to see how he kept the promises he made in the past (See overview paragraphs 1–2 and 5).

   Bible references: Joshua 1:2-6; 24:3, 5, 8; Genesis 15:13-14; Matthew 1:21-23.
   Questions: How does it feel when you know you can trust someone to keep their promises? Do you know that you can feel that way about God?

2. God punished Jericho and Ai severely for their sin, because although God is patient, he will not put up with sin forever (See overview paragraphs 3–5).

   Bible references: Joshua 23:12-13, 15-16; Numbers 14:18; Galatians 6:7-8.
   Questions: How did God punish the sins of the people of Jericho? How did he punish the sins of the *Israelites*? How do you think God feels about sin?

3. God made his people to be *holy* – separate from the nations around them, because those nations worshiped false gods and behaved badly. *Circumcision* was a sign that God's people were separate. God wants us to be separate now, and to show that we are separate by obeying him, rather than just doing what everyone else is doing (See overview paragraphs 2–5).

   Bible references: Joshua 23:7-8, 12-13; Genesis 17: 10, 14; 2 Corinthians 6:16-17.
   Questions: What do you see or hear at school, online or on TV that shows how people don't love God? If you are going to be separate and not just do what everyone else does, what things will you not do? What kinds of things do you think you will do?

SALVATION THREAD

Getting to the *promised land* and making it their home was one of the most important events in the history of Israel. It showed them they were God's special people, and that God kept his promises, loved them, protected and blessed them.

If we believe in Jesus and put our trust in him, then we too have a *promised land* to look forward to that God promises us: *heaven*. Jesus is making it ready for us (John 14:1–3), and one day we will go there to be with him forever. There will be no deep rivers to cross, no enemies to fight and no danger of disobeying God when we are there. God will have made us perfect when it is time to be in heaven, and we will be in perfect peace with him.

Key Verse: "Be strong and courageous. Do not be terrified; do not be discouraged, for the LORD your God will be with you wherever you go" (Joshua 1:9).

The book of
JUDGES

JUDGES

Rebellion, rescue, rebellion, rescue ... repeat ...

INTRODUCTION

- Judges is full of Israel rejecting God, followed by getting attacked by their enemies and then crying out to God. Again and again and again. Each time, God rescued them, using heroes and amazing victories. Those heroes were leaders of Israel, called 'Judges'. The action in the book of Judges happens over 400 years, after the people arrived and made their homes in the *promised land*, and before they asked for a king. Samuel, the last of the Judges to rule over Israel, may have written this book.

- The events in this book probably happened between 1350 and 1080 B.C.

OVERVIEW

1. "After Joshua died, the tribes of Judah and Simeon won many battles. However, the *Israelites* were not able to drive out the people living in the country, and were also starting to be attacked. God told Israel this was because they had been disobedient to him. The Israelites after Joshua's time didn't know God or what he had done for his people, and they started worshiping false gods."

2. "During this time, God raised up fourteen leaders, many of whom were called 'judges'. They saved the people from their enemies, ruled over God's people and reminded them to obey God. When each judge led the country, the people obeyed God until the judge died, and then the people usually forgot about God again and started disobeying him. Even the Judges were sometimes disobedient to God."

3. "One of the judges was called Gideon – an unimportant man from a small tribe, but God chose him to lead Israel. God defeated a massive army of over 120,000 Midianites using Gideon's army of only 300 soldiers."

4. "Samson was a judge, and God gave him amazing strength. He killed a lion without any help or weapons, and he killed lots of God's enemies. But after a while he thought his great strength was his own, instead of a gift from God, so God took his strength away. The Philistines, who were Israel's enemies, captured Samson. When he attacked the Philistines for the last time, he said '*O God, please strengthen me just once more.*'[11] God said yes to his prayer and the Philistines were defeated."

5. "The people of Israel just kept doing what they wanted, disobeying God and doing terrible things to each other."

---

11. Judges 16:28.

LEARNING FROM JUDGES

1. God was patient with Israel. They forgot about him many times, but he didn't forget them. He kept on rescuing them from their enemies and reminding them that they needed to worship and obey only him. God is patient with you. He reminds you that you need to worship and obey only him (See overview paragraphs 1–2 and 5).

   Bible references: Judges 3:7; Psalm 78:7-8; 2 Peter 3:9.

   Questions: How many leaders are there in this book? How many times did the people disobey God? How impatient do you get when people are nasty to you? Imagine if God was like that every time we disobey him!

2. The *Israelites* went to war against their enemies, but only God could save them. Our great enemy is *sin*. We try to obey God but only he can give us the strength to do it. Only he can forgive our sins (See overview paragraphs 1, 3–4).

   Bible references: Judges 6:3-4, 6; 7:2-3; Psalm 59:16; Matthew 19:26.

   Question: What did your parents do for you when you were a baby? What do they do for you now? Are you trusting God for the things only he can do?

3. Sometimes God does amazing things called miracles to show he is real and that we need only him (See overview paragraphs 3–4).

   Bible references: Judges 14:5-6; Exodus 8:22; John 6:19; 20:31.

   Questions: What miracles did God do with Gideon and Samson? What are some of the miracles that Jesus did?

SALVATION THREAD

Gideon seemed unimportant to the people around him (6:15), but God chose him to be a judge, a leader of all Israel, and to win an amazing battle. When Gideon gathered an army of 32,000 to fight the Midianites, God made 31,700 go back home, leaving only 300 of them to fight a much bigger army. God wanted to show that it was God's strength that would defeat the enemy.

When Jesus came to earth, people didn't think he looked important. He was a normal looking man, doing a job as a carpenter in a town people thought was no good. Gideon is a picture of Jesus. In God's strength Gideon saved a country from their enemies. Jesus saved all God's people in history from the biggest enemy: *sin*.

Key Verse: "I brought you up out of Egypt and led you into the land that I swore to give to your forefathers. I said, 'I will never break my covenant with you … Yet you have disobeyed me. Why have you done this?'" (Judges 2:1-2).

The book of

RUTH

RUTH

Everything works out according to God's plan

INTRODUCTION

- God does things his way – the perfect way. It's not always what we would think of, and it's not always with people who look like heroes. For example, Ruth was not an Israelite. She was from Moab, which was often fighting with Israel. Her husband had died, and she was very poor. Yet God chose her to be in the family line of King David, and of Jesus himself.

- Ruth returned home to Israel in about 1100 B.C.

OVERVIEW

4. "When Naomi heard that God had provided food for his people back in Israel, she told Orpah and Ruth to stay in Moab while she went back to Israel. However, Ruth said, '*Where you go I will go … Your people will be my people and your God my God,*'[12] so she went with Naomi."

5. "Back in Israel, Naomi had an important relative called Boaz. Because Naomi and Ruth were so poor, Ruth collected spare grain for food, in a field belonging to Boaz. When Boaz noticed Ruth, and found out that they were related, he let her gather grain in his field whenever she wanted. He even made sure extra grain was left for her and gave her extra food because of all that she had done to stay with and look after Naomi."

6. "After a while, Naomi said Ruth should see if Boaz would marry her. He was an older man, but he was part of Naomi's family. It would keep the family name going if Ruth and Boaz had children together, and Naomi knew that was a good thing. Boaz agreed to marry Ruth, even though it cost him money and land to do so, and they had a son."

7. "'*Praise be to the* LORD,'" said the women in Bethlehem, '*for he has given you a son to rescue your family – your daughter-in-law [Ruth] who loves you and who is better to you than seven sons, has given him birth.*'[13]

8. "Boaz and Ruth's child was called Obed. *He was the father of Jesse, the father of David*" who became King.[14]

---

12. Ruth 1:16.
13. Ruth 4:14-15.
14. Ruth 4:17. That wasn't just any David, but the David who went on to become King of Israel.

LEARNING FROM RUTH

1. God's people are not special because of what they've done; they are special because God loves them. Ruth was not even an Israelite – she was a Moabite and was likely to stay poor and without a husband for the rest of her life. But God had other plans for her, giving her a husband and placing her in the family line of King David and of Jesus (See overview paragraphs 1, 3–4).

   Bible references: Ruth 4:13-14; Deuteronomy 9:6; Titus 3:4-5.

   Questions: Why do the people around you think they are special? What is special about you?

2. Boaz "redeemed" Ruth's family by marrying her and buying the land that would have belonged to Ruth's husband, who died. To "redeem" is to get something back (usually with money) for yourself or someone else that used to belong to them but had been taken away. Boaz ended up with less land and less money because he redeemed Ruth's family, paying for their land, but he was happy to do it. Jesus paid with his life to redeem his people from *sin*, but he did it willingly (See overview paragraph 4).

   Bible references: Ruth 3:11-13; 2 Samuel 7:23; Romans 3:24.

   Question: What is most special to you? If it were lost, how much would you give to "redeem" it (buy it back)? If God gave his life to redeem his people, how special do you think they are to him?

3. The book of Ruth is full of kindness, such as God's to Ruth, Ruth's to Naomi, Boaz's to Ruth (See overview paragraphs 2–5).

   Bible references: Ruth 2:11-12, 19-20; Genesis 32:10; Ephesians 2:7.

   Questions: How did God, Boaz and Ruth show their kindness? How has God shown you kindness? How can you show kindness to other people?

SALVATION THREAD

God shows us the family links of his son Jesus. He tells us who Jesus is, to help us know that Jesus is a real man from a real family.

Look at the verses below, that match each other. Remember that Matthew was written well over 1,000 years after the events in Ruth. What God did through Ruth was all part of his promise to send a Savior who would come from the family line of King David.

"Boaz the father of Obed, Obed the father of Jesse, and Jesse the father of David" (Ruth 4:21-22).

"Boaz, the father of Obed, whose mother was Ruth, Obed the father of Jesse, and Jesse the father of King David … [15] and Jacob the father of Joseph, the husband of Mary, of whom was born Jesus, who is called Christ" (Matthew 1:5-6, 16).

Key Verse: "Don't urge me to leave you or to turn back from you. Where you go I will go, and where you stay I will stay. Your people will be my people and your God my God" (Ruth 1:16).

---

15. The dots refer to there being many generations – and about 500 years - between David and Jacob that are not listed here, for the sake of space.

The books of
1 & 2 SAMUEL

1 SAMUEL

The kingdom begins

INTRODUCTION

- Battles, the first King of Israel and a manhunt that went on for years. That's what is going on in this book. At the start we have the birth of Samuel and at the end the death of Saul. Samuel was the last of the judges to lead Israel, and he anointed the first two kings. Samuel is a key character of this book, and he may have written most of it.

- The events of 1 Samuel happened between 1100 and 1000 B.C.

OVERVIEW

1. "Hannah couldn't have babies, but she kept on praying to God and God gave her a son called Samuel. Samuel worked for God his whole life, and God made him a *prophet*. During this time the *Israelites* were worshiping false gods and didn't listen to God. But after the *Philistines* defeated them in battle the *Israelites* repented, throwing away their false gods."

2. "The *Philistines* kept attacking, but God defeated them to rescue his people. However, when Samuel was old the people asked for a king so that they could be like other countries who had kings. They didn't trust God. God said it would be bad for them, but they wouldn't listen, so God gave them the kind of king they wanted – a big man, called Saul."

3. "Samuel told the Israelites to remember everything God had done for them, and obey him. '*Do not turn away [to] useless idols. They can do you no good, nor can they rescue you,*'[16] he said."

4. "God gave Saul a desire to serve and love God, but Saul didn't stay like that, and started to disobey God in many ways. After a while Samuel said to Saul, '*Because you have rejected the word of the LORD, he has rejected you as king.*'[17] God said that a young man called David would be king instead. God's Spirit came on David in power. David, who wasn't very big, killed a giant Philistine called Goliath with just a leather strap called a sling which he used to throw a stone onto the giant's head. David then won lots of battles against Israel's enemies, and people liked him more than Saul."

5. "Saul became jealous and tried to kill David, though Saul's son Jonathan was David's best friend. David ran away to hide, and stayed away for a long time. Twice he had a chance to kill Saul, but because God had made Saul king, David didn't want to hurt Saul."

---

16. 1 Samuel 12:21.
17. 1 Samuel 15:23.

6. "After forty-two years as king, Saul and three of his sons died when they lost a battle against the *Philistines*."

LEARNING FROM 1 SAMUEL

1. It is easy to stop trusting God and to trust ourselves or others. Even after the *Israelites* had repented, they forgot about God and stopped trusting him. Remember that God is the Almighty God who has done great things and knows what is best (See overview paragraphs 1–2).

   Bible references: 1 Samuel 8:7-8; 12:21; Proverbs 3:5-6; 2 Corinthians 1:9.

   Questions: How did God show the Israelites that he was their Almighty God who could and should always be trusted? What amazing things has God done to show you can always trust him to be most powerful and wise?

2. God is in command of history. It was God who answered Hannah's prayer for a child. It was God who told Samuel to appoint Saul and then David to be king. God removed Saul so that one day David could become king (See overview paragraphs 1–2 and 4).

   Bible references: 1 Samuel 2:6–7; Isaiah 45:7; Matthew 8:27.

   Question: Look at all the things that happen in 1 Samuel, both good and bad. God uses all those things for his glory. What does that tell us that God is like? What does it say about how powerful he is?

3. When God's power is with people, there is nothing they cannot do. When God's power is not with people, they can't do anything. David had no training to be a soldier, but he killed the giant Philistine called Goliath. When Saul rejected God, he lost everything (See overview paragraphs 4 and 6).

   Bible references: 1 Samuel 15:26; 16:13; 1 Chronicles 29:12; Ephesians 6:10-11.

   Question: Imagine trying to turn on a computer with no electricity, or a car with no fuel. That's like trying to obey God without his help – it doesn't work.

SALVATION THREAD

In the Old Testament there are prophets, priests and kings. No-one in the Old Testament had been all three of those things at the same time. Even the really famous people in the history of Israel were mostly just one of those things. Samuel was such a key person because he was two: *prophet* and *priest*, as well as being the leader.

Samuel points us to the one man – the perfect Jew – who was all three of those things: Jesus. He is the *priest*, talking to God the Father for his people. He is the *prophet*, bringing God's message of hope. And he is the king of all creation.

Key Verse: "For the sake of his great name the LORD will not reject his people, because the LORD was pleased to make you his own" (1 Samuel 12:22).

2 SAMUEL

A promise from God that last forever

INTRODUCTION

- David's life was a rollercoaster. As king he united his country, defeated his enemies and God made him some amazing promises. But David also sinned greatly and his son Absalom launched a war against him. Originally 1 and 2 Samuel were the same book, but some of the first people to translate the Bible decided to divide them into two parts. Whoever wrote this book probably lived soon after the death of King Solomon, David's son.

- The events of 2 Samuel happened between 1000 and 950 B.C.

OVERVIEW

1. "After the death of Saul and Jonathan, David became king first over the southern part of the country, and after a few years and some battles, over the north as well. He was king over the whole country between the ages of thirty-seven and seventy. Whenever Israel's enemies attacked, God gave David's army victory."

2. "God promised that he would make David important and famous and give him protection from his enemies. He said that God's people would have a home and peace, and that David's son would be king after him. '*Your house and your kingdom shall endure forever before me; your throne shall be established forever*,'[18] God said. David was amazed and said, '*How great you are, O Sovereign Lord! There is no-one like you, and there is no God but you …*'"[19]

3. "David was a good king and fair with his people. However, he also did some very bad things. Once he took another man's wife, called Bathsheba, to be his own, and put her husband in a dangerous place in a battle so that he was killed. David and Bathsheba's first son then died. David didn't even realize how bad he had been until God's *prophet* called Nathan told him; then David was sorry and asked God to forgive him."

4. "Some awful things happened in David's family as well. David's son Absalom ran away and David wouldn't forgive him or speak to him. After a few years Absalom tried to take David's place as king but was defeated by David's armies and killed. That led to another rebellion against David, but David's army won that battle as well."

5. "When David was old he wanted to know how many men in the country could fight, instead of just trusting in God who had always given him victory. God was angry at David's lack of *faith* and the whole country was punished – many people died. David was sorry to God for his lack of *faith*, and wished that he was being punished instead of the people."

---

18. 2 Samuel 7:16.
19. 2 Samuel 7:22.

LEARNING FROM 2 SAMUEL

1. God's promise to David was one of the covenants that we read about in the Old Testament. David was right to be amazed at how wonderful God had been to him. It reminded him to worship God as the one true God. We too should worship God when we think of all he has done for us (See overview paragraph 2).

    Bible references: 2 Samuel 7:9-12, 16; 1 Kings 8:20; Revelation 22:16.

    Questions: What has God done for you? Can you think of some small and big things he has done? What is the most important thing God has done for you?

2. No-one except Jesus is perfect. Even King David, who God loved, wasn't perfect. When we sin, we should do what David did and *repent* of our sins, asking God to forgive us (See overview paragraphs 3–5).

    Bible references: 2 Samuel 22:31-32; Psalm 51; 1 John 1:9.

    Questions: How do you feel when you do something sinful? Do you feel like God can't forgive you? Remember that God loves to forgive sins.

3. *Sin* causes death in the world and separation from God forever. However, God has defeated *sin* and death through Jesus and offers life with him to all those who *repent* (See overview paragraphs 3 and 5).

    Bible references: 2 Samuel 12:9-10, 13-14; Genesis 3:3; Romans 6:13.

    Questions: What were some of the bad things that David did? If God forgave David the wrong things that he did, do you think that God can forgive you? Would you like him to do that?

SALVATION THREAD

When God made his promise to David he said that his son would become king after him, and that, "Your house and your kingdom shall endure for ever before me; your throne shall be established for ever" (2 Samuel 7:16). David's son Solomon did become king, but God was mainly talking about the one who would be king forever: Jesus.

The *apostle* Paul said about God, that "After removing Saul, he made David their king. He testified concerning him: 'I have found David son of Jesse a man after my own heart; he will do everything I want him to do'. From this man's descendants God has brought to Israel the Savior Jesus, as he promised" (Acts 13:22-23). Jesus even describes himself in Revelation 22:16, as "the Root, and the Offspring of David".

Many times during his life on earth, people called Jesus the "Son of David", meaning the one who comes after David, from David's family, who would save Israel (Matthew 1:1 and 17). David had been the most glorious king in the history of Israel, but God's people looked forward to the day when the perfect 'Son of David' would come.

Some of the *Israelites* thought God would just send them a great soldier to defeat their enemies, but what God was promising was something much more important. He was getting ready to send the one who would save them from their sins and bring them back into a good relationship with him.

Key Verse: "He gives his king great victories; he shows unfailing kindness to his anointed, to David and his descendants for ever" (2 Samuel 22:51).

The books of
1 & 2 KINGS

1 KINGS

When leadership goes wrong

INTRODUCTION

- Israel had some of its most glorious years during the reign of King David, but the kings who came after him got very bad, very quickly. 1 and 2 Kings are really two parts of the same book, taking us from the last days of David to the *exile* in Babylon. It is a history of God dealing with his people through the kings of Judah and Israel. (David and Solomon ruled over the whole of Israel, but after Solomon it was divided into the tribe of Judah and the rest of Israel.) 1 Kings covers about 130 years of history, and we don't know who wrote it.

- The events of 1 Kings happened between 950 and 850 B.C.

OVERVIEW

1. "When David was old he made his son Solomon king. When God said he could have anything he wanted, Solomon asked for wisdom so that he could be a good king for God. God was pleased with this and made him wise as he asked, and also very rich. The country was at peace and the people were happy. Solomon built an amazing *temple* for God full of gold that took seven years to build, and he then spent thirteen years building an amazing palace for himself."

2. "Twice, God promised wonderful blessings if Solomon would keep obeying him, but terrible things if he disobeyed. After a while, Solomon disobeyed God by marrying hundreds of women and starting to worship false gods. As punishment for this, God said that Solomon's son would not be king of the whole country, and there would not be peace any more."

3. "After Solomon died, his son was mean to the people so they made Jereboam king of most of the country instead, leaving Solomon's son Rehoboam with only his own tribe of Judah to rule over. But Jereboam started to worship other gods and encouraged the people to do the same, so God didn't let Jereboam's family keep ruling Israel."

4. "Later, King Ahab ruled and was more evil than all the other kings of Israel before him. He worshiped a false god called Baal. Ahab was eventually killed in battle."

5. "Ahab's wife, Jezebel, killed many of God's prophets. One day, the prophet Elijah challenged the false prophets to ask their gods to burn up a *sacrifice*. They asked loudly all day but couldn't do it. Elijah asked God to burn up the *sacrifice* and God did it by sending fire from *heaven* (he even burnt all the water!). The people saw that God is the one true God."

LEARNING FROM 1 KINGS

1. For a while when Solomon became king, he wanted to love and obey God. God blessed him and the Israelites with peace and they had enough of everything they needed. God loves to bless his people (See overview paragraphs 1–2).

   Bible references: 1 Kings 8:23; 9:4-5; Psalms 29:11; Ephesians 1:3.
   Questions: How did God bless Solomon and the whole country? And you? If God said you could have anything you wanted, what would you ask for?

2. God punishes those who disobey him (See overview paragraphs 2–4).

   Bible references: 1 Kings 11:9-12; Numbers 14:18; 2 Thessalonians 1:8.
   Questions: How did Solomon, Rehoboam, Jeroboam and Ahab disobey God? Do you worship God as he commands?

3. God is the one true God and is the only one who must be worshiped. Elijah proved that God is the only real, living God. It is most important that we remember that. (See overview paragraphs 2–5).

   Bible references: 1 Kings 18:38-39; 22:53; Isaiah 43:10-11; John 20:28-31.
   Questions: How did God use Elijah to prove that God is real, and that Baal was not real? How did God punish those who worshiped false gods?

SALVATION THREAD

The *Israelites* could see their suffering was not because God didn't care, or wasn't strong enough to help. It was because of their *sin* – they had broken their *covenant* with God. Not just once, they were sinning and not caring about it. If they would *repent* of their sins then God would again bless them.

When we read this book we can see how faithful, loving and patient God is. Most of the kings disobeyed him and the people worshiped false gods, so God kept his promise to punish them. However, he also kept his covenant with them – his promise to send a Savior who would save his people from their sins.

1 Kings helps us to see that God keeping his promise doesn't depend on anything except God's own faithfulness, and we can praise God that he "is faithful to all his promises."[20]

Key Verse: "Lord, the God of Israel, there is no God like you in heaven above or on earth below—you who keep your covenant of love with your servants who continue wholeheartedly in your way" (1 Kings 8:23).

---

20. Psalm 145:13.

2 KINGS

From disobedience to defeat

INTRODUCTION

- Have you ever warned someone of danger? Were they about to touch something hot, or tread on something sharp? You might feel like warning the *Israelites* in 2 Kings as they continued in disobedience against God. 2 Kings is the second part of the history of God's dealing with his people through the lives of the kings of Judah and Israel.[21] The book covers about 250 years of history. We don't know who wrote it.

- The events of 2 Kings happened between 850 and 600 B.C.

OVERVIEW

1. "Elijah was taken straight to heaven in a whirlwind – he didn't die! Elisha took over from Elijah as God's messenger to the people. God did many amazing things through Elisha, including bringing a dead boy back to life and healing a man from a horrible disease called leprosy."

2. "Most of the kings of Israel and Judah, along with the rest of the country, didn't want to obey God, and worshiped false gods. As punishment, God made Israel smaller through enemies taking over some of the towns. God rescued Israel from their enemies many times, to show them that they needed to turn back to him, but they didn't listen."

3. "After many more warnings, God used the Assyrians to punish Israel by beating Israel in war and taking many of the people as prisoners."

4. "Judah, the other part of God's people, then had a good king, Hezekiah, who trusted and worshiped God. He helped the people to do the same and God blessed him. When Judah was attacked by a much bigger army, and were told by their enemies that God couldn't help, God saved them."

5. "After King Hezekiah came King Manasseh, who did many evil things and led the people to worship false gods. Later, when Josiah was king, someone found God's book,[22] which nobody had read for a long time. It was read to Josiah who saw how important it was to obey and worship God, so he read it to the people."

6. "However, God still needed to punish Judah because they refused to repent, and the Babylonians beat them in war. Many people died and many others were taken away

---

21. The nation of God's people – Israel – was split and became two nations: Israel in the north and Judah in the south. Each nation had its own king.
22. The passage in 2 Kings 22-23 refers to 'The Book of the Law', which means the first five books of what we call The Bible: Genesis, Exodus, Leviticus, Numbers, Deuteronomy. For the people at the time, that was the whole of The Bible because the reset was not yet written.

from their homes or ran away to a different country. All because God's people had turned away from God."

LEARNING FROM 2 KINGS

1. God was patient with the people of Israel and Judah, wanting them to come back to him. God is patient with us too, and wants us to be sorry for our sins so that we can be forgiven (See overview paragraphs 2 and 4).

   Bible references: 2 Kings 21:15; 2 Peter 3:9; 1 Timothy 1:16.

   Questions: What bad things were God's people doing? What did God do, to remind them that they needed to turn back to him?

2. Sin is evil, and God will punish it. If we do not want to obey God, and do not want his forgiveness we will be without God forever (See overview paragraphs 3 and 6).

   Bible references: 2 Kings 22:16-17; Nehemiah 9:30; 2 Peter 3:7.

   Question: Do you think that disobeying God is a big deal? Why, or why not?

3. Judah had kings such as Hezekiah and Josiah who helped them to love God and his Word. Thank God for people who show us the Bible, and show us how to love God (See overview paragraphs 4–5).

   Bible references: 2 Kings 22:8-10; 23:2-3; Ephesians 6:4; 2 Timothy 1:5.

   Questions: Who tells you about God? You could tell someone about loving God.

SALVATION THREAD

"When Athaliah the mother of Ahaziah saw that her son was dead, she proceeded to destroy the whole royal family. But Jehosheba, the daughter of King Jehoram and sister of Ahaziah, took Joash son of Ahaziah and stole him away from among the royal princes, who were about to be murdered. She put him and his nurse in a bedroom to hide him from Athaliah; so he was not killed" (2 Kings 11:1-2).

God promised that the Messiah – Jesus – would come from King David's family (2 Samuel 7:16). However, Athaliah tried to have all the people from that family killed. If she succeeded, God's plan for the coming of Jesus would have failed. But God is God and his plans never fail. He knew what Athaliah would try to do, and he stopped her from doing what she wanted. He kept one member of the family alive, who went on to have children and so the family survived. 800 years later, Jesus was born from that family.

Key Verse: "Now I know that there is no God in all the world except in Israel" (2 Kings 5:15).

The books of
1 & 2 CHRONICLES

1 CHRONICLES

Thousands of years of history in one book

INTRODUCTION

- Going through Chronicles is like going in a rocket through history. A chronicle is a story of important things that really happened, written down in order. Chronicles was originally one book, divided into two by people who translated the Bible into English. We don't know who wrote it, but it may have been the *priest* Ezra. Lots of the information in Chronicles comes from different places and other books, including Kings and Samuel. The first book of Chronicles tells us about people from Adam and Eve through to King David.

- 1 Chronicles was probably written about 450 B.C.

OVERVIEW

1. "Adam was the first person on earth. He had a son called Seth, who had a son called Enosh, who had a son called Kenan." The family list goes on like that, including Noah, Abraham, Jacob, and Jacob's sons. (Jacob's sons became the twelve parts of Israel, called tribes, who lived in the *promised land* after God rescued them from Egypt.) The list of people keeps going on to King David, and the other kings of Judah (a part of Israel) who came after him.

2. "Saul was the first king of Israel but he disobeyed God, so God made him lose in battle and replaced him with a man called David, who became King of all Israel, including Judah."

3. "God promised that he would make David's kingdom last forever, and that his son would build a temple for God."

4. "King David made sure he did what God wanted, and God gave him success in battle against the enemies of God's people. However, one day David started thinking all his victories were because of him and not God, so God brought a terrible punishment on the country. David was sorry to God, and God forgave him and stopped the punishment."

5. "David then started to get ready to build the temple, getting wood and stone and other things that were needed. He also gave different jobs to the men in the tribe of Levi – it was their job to look after the temple when it was built, and some of them would be priests."

6. "King David praised God, and told his son Solomon to make sure that he obeyed God and worked hard for God. He reminded Solomon that God would bless him if

he obeyed, but would reject him if he did not obey. Then King David died and Solomon became king."

LEARNING FROM 1 CHRONICLES

1. The lists of names at the beginning of 1 Chronicles reminds us that the Bible is not a book of made-up stories, it has stories about real people, and what God did through them and with them. (See overview paragraph 1).

    Bible references: 1 Chronicles 8:40–9:1; Nehemiah 7:6-7; Luke 3:23-24.

    Questions: Some of the people in the 1 Chronicles family list are Adam, Noah and Abraham. Can you remember anything about those men from the Bible? (Look at chapters 1a and 1b of this book.)

2. Sometimes when we are having a good time, we think that we deserve it, or we forget that good times are a gift from God. That's what David did. Remember: everything good comes from God; he gives us good things even though we don't deserve them (See overview paragraphs 2 and 3).

    Bible references: 1 Chronicles 18:13b; Psalm 103:10; James 1:17.

    Questions: What good things do you have? What good things do you enjoy doing? Do you have and do those things because you are good, or because God has given them to you?

3. We must obey God. But God knows that just like King David, we cannot be perfect. That is why the first command to obey is to be sorry for our sins and ask God to forgive us (See overview paragraphs 2 and 4).

    Bible references: 1 Chronicles 21:17, 26; Ezekiel 14:6; Acts 20:21.

    Questions: Do you always do the right thing? Have you asked God to forgive you for the times you don't?

SALVATION THREAD

"I will raise up your offspring to succeed you, one of your own sons, and I will establish his kingdom. He is the one who will build a house for me, and I will establish his throne forever. I will be his father, and he will be my son. I will never take my love away from him, as I took it away from your predecessor. I will set him over my house and my kingdom forever; his throne will be established for ever" (1 Chronicles 17:11-14).

"… to which of the angels did God ever say, 'You are my Son; today I have become your Father'? Or again, 'I will be his Father and he will be my Son'?" (Hebrews 1:5).

The writer of Hebrews was talking about how Jesus is even greater than the angels. He also showed that the above words from 1 Chronicles were first talking about Solomon, but they were also a prophecy talking about Jesus. Solomon was an important man, but just a man; Jesus was and is the Son of God.

Key Verse: "Look to the Lord and his strength; seek his face always. Remember the wonders he has done, his miracles, and the judgments he pronounced" (1 Chronicles 16:11-12).

2 CHRONICLES

A country heads for disaster because of sin ... but God still loves them

---

INTRODUCTION

- Have you ever felt like you're heading for trouble? During the history in this book, Israel was heading for trouble. The early days of King Solomon were a peaceful and happy time, but through the next nineteen kings of Judah things got worse and worse. Then there was the *exile* to Babylon and seventy years after that, the return to Judah.

- 2 Chronicles was probably written about 450 B.C.

OVERVIEW

1. "When Solomon asked for wisdom so he could be a good king, God made him the wisest person in the world, and also made him very rich. Solomon built a huge and beautiful *temple* using many workers. When it was finished, Solomon prayed that God would forgive the *Israelites* for their sins when they were sorry for them, so that people everywhere would know who God is and give him respect."

2. "After Solomon, his son Rehoboam became king. Rehoboam told the people he would be nasty, to make them work even harder than before. That sounded bad so ten of the tribes decided to make a man called Jereboam king instead. Just two of the tribes stayed with Rehoboam."

3. "So, instead of being just one country from this time they were split in two. The ten tribes were known as Israel, while the two tribes (Judah and Benjamin) were known as Judah. For many years they fought against each other."

4. "Some of the kings of Judah who came later, obeyed God and looked to him for help. When they did that, God gave them success and the people had peace. Others disobeyed God, and for them there was no peace."

5. "King Manasseh of Judah was evil, and ignored God's warnings. So God punished him by letting his enemies beat him in war and take him away. Then Manasseh repented of his sins, and God brought him back to Judah to be king again."

6. "Most of the kings of Judah after Manasseh were evil. God sent messages through the prophets that the king and people must *repent*, but they laughed at the messages and treated the prophets badly. In the end, God punished Judah in a big way. The country was destroyed in war and many people were taken away to a different country, called Babylon."

7. "After seventy years, the people of Judah were allowed to go back home, just as God said would happen."

LEARNING FROM 2 CHRONICLES

1. God was patient with his people. During the period of the kings they had disobeyed God for about 300 years, before he punished them. They were taken 'into *exile*': away from their homes, away from their country. God is patient with us, too – we all have the opportunity to turn to God and be sorry for our sins (See overview paragraph 6).

   Bible references: 2 Chronicles 35:18;[23] 1 Samuel 8:7-8; Nehemiah 9:30; 2 Peter 3:9.
   Questions: If someone is being mean to you, how long does it take before you want them to be punished? How would you feel if God was like that with you?

2. Nobody is so bad that God will not forgive their sins if they *repent*. King Manasseh worshiped false gods, built places for other people to worship false gods, and murdered many people including his own sons. But he repented, and God forgave him (See overview paragraph 5).

   Bible references: 2 Chronicles 33:1-2; 1 Corinthians 5:9; 2 Corinthians 6:2.
   Question: Do you sometimes think that God does not want to forgive you? If God forgave Manasseh, do you think he will forgive you if you ask him to?

3. God doesn't stand still waiting for people to repent. He tells them and shows them many times and in different ways, what they need to do. The problem is not that people don't know they need to repent; the problem is that they don't want to repent (See overview paragraphs 5–6).

   Bible references: 2 Chronicles 36:15-16; Isaiah 46:12-13; Romans 1:18-19.
   Question: Do you want to repent? Have you done that?

SALVATION THREAD

Chronicles was written for all of God's people who came back after exile – they needed to be encouraged that God's promises were still in place. Chronicles showed them:

- The family line from King David was still there (as God promised it would be).

- God's people were able to come back to their own country after seventy years away (as God promised they would).

- The *temple* would be rebuilt (for God to live in as he promised he would).

So God's biggest promise of all – that someone from David's family who would save his people from their sins – was still on course. It would still happen at the right time. Nothing could stop it – not even the sinfulness of God's people, or the enemies who defeated them and took them into *exile*.

Key Verse: "… the LORD your God is gracious and compassionate. He will not turn his face from you if you return to him" (2 Chronicles 30:9).

---

23. God told the Jews that every year they should celebrate Passover. It was a celebration of when God kept them safe from the plague of death that came on Egypt, while all the Jews were slaves in that country. However, the kings before Josiah disobeyed: they did not hold the Passover celebration.

The book of

EZRA

EZRA

God's people returned from exile, but the persecution continued

INTRODUCTION

- Home at last! After seventy years, the Jews who were *exiled* to Babylon were allowed to return to Judah. But how did this happen? King Nebuchadnezzar, who invaded Judah and took the people to Babylon, was defeated. The Persians took over Babylon and it was the Persian king who allowed the Jews to make the 900-mile walk back home. But even then, their troubles were not over. Ezra the priest wrote about it.

- The events of Ezra happened from 537 to 515 B.C. and 458 to about 433 B.C.

OVERVIEW

1. "To keep his promise that his people would come home, God made King Cyrus of Persia know that God is real, and that the Jews should be allowed to go home to Israel. Cyrus gave back to the Jews all the things that the Babylonians had stolen from the *temple*. Nearly 50,000 people returned to Israel, including people from Bethlehem, and priests and servants."

2. "When the Jews got back they built an altar to God, so they could worship and make sacrifices to him. They started to rebuild the *temple*, which was knocked down by the Babylonians seventy years earlier. The *Israelites* were so happy, and sang to God: 'He is good; his love to Israel goes on forever.'"[24]

3. "Some people from other countries pretended to be friends of the Jews and offered to help. But when the Jews said no thanks, the foreigners were mean to the Jews in order to stop them building the *temple*."

4. "Later, King Xerxes of Persia forced the Jews to stop building – he was afraid that if they got too powerful they would fight against him. The Jews though, helped and encouraged by the prophets Haggai and Zechariah, started building again and finished the *temple*. When they finished they celebrated the Passover."

5. "Before that, Ezra led the second group of Jews home, sixty years after the first group. God was with Ezra because he worked hard to honour God, to understand, obey and teach the Bible."

6. "Then Ezra was told that many men who came home to Israel, disobeyed God badly. They married women from other countries who didn't love God at all. Ezra was extremely sad and prayed to God asking for forgiveness for the people. When they saw Ezra like that, the people realized they had done wrong and they were very sorry to God."

---

24. Ezra 3:11.

LEARNING FROM EZRA

1. God's people were allowed to go home, just as he promised and just when he said they would. Thank God that he keeps all his promises (See overview paragraph 1).

   Bible references: Ezra 1:1; Jeremiah 25:12; John 4:53.

   Questions: What did God do to King Cyrus to keep his promise? How can you see God in action today?

2. When the Jews got back to their country, they were going to build big walls as protection from their enemies. But first they built an altar for a sacrifice to God. They were so thankful to God for letting them go home. They knew that worshiping God was more important than a good wall for their town (See overview paragraph 2).

   Bible references: Ezra 3:3; Exodus 4:31; Acts 2:42.

   Question: Is it important to you to worship God? The more we love God, the more we will want to worship God with God's people (for example at church).

3. If we fill our lives with things that God likes, it helps us to love and obey God properly, which is the most important thing. That's why it was so bad that the men married women who didn't love God (See overview paragraph 6).

   Bible references: Ezra 9:1-4; 1 Corinthians 7:39; 2 Corinthians 6:14.

   Question: What can you do, read, or say that God likes, and makes it easier to obey him? What could you do, read or say that would make it more difficult to love and obey God?

SALVATION THREAD

God doesn't just watch history happening - he makes it happen. The whole Bible is the story of what God has done, not just what people have done. Ezra 1:1 tells us that, "the LORD moved the heart of Cyrus king of Persia" to let the Jews go back home. Cyrus wouldn't have done that on his own, God made it happen.

Later, another king called Darius helped make sure the Jews could finish the *temple*, after some people tried to stop them. The Jews then "… celebrated with joy … because the LORD had filled them with joy by changing the attitude of the king of Assyria [Darius], so that he assisted them in the work on the house of God" (Ezra 6:22).

We see another example of God making things happen in the New Testament, we read that "the Lord opened [Lydia's] heart to respond to Paul's message" (Acts 16:14) about Jesus' free offer of forgiveness. And there are many other examples.

God is doing the same thing now. If we are saved from our sins, it is because God has saved us, not because we are good enough or clever enough to do it ourselves.

Key Verses: "… the gracious hand of his God was on him. For Ezra had devoted himself to the study and observance of the *Law* of the LORD, and to teaching its decrees and laws in Israel" (Ezra 7:9-10).

The book of
NEHEMIAH

NEHEMIAH

God's people were going home

INTRODUCTION

- God's people were back in their country, and already people wanted to attack them! Zerubbabel led the first group back from Babylon in about the year 537 B.C., and then Ezra led the second group in about 458 B.C. Nehemiah returned in about 445 B.C., and went back to Babylon for a while before returning to Israel for the rest of his life. He knew Ezra, who wrote most of the book of Nehemiah, though it included many of Nehemiah's own words.

- The events of this book happened from 445 to 444 B.C. and 433 to 432 B.C.

OVERVIEW

1. "I [Nehemiah] was still in Babylon and found out that the Jews went back to Israel were having a bad time. This made me sad, so I prayed to God about it. Then, thank God, the king let me go back to Israel for a while to help rebuild the country."

2. "When I got back I encouraged people to start building. Almost everyone joined in and the work went very well."

3. "However, one of the nearby leaders, called Sanballat, didn't want God's people to do well. He laughed at us and was angry. We found out that he was bringing an army to attack, so all the people working on the wall started carrying a sword with them, just in case."

4. "Then we had a problem because the rich people were making the poor people pay too much money. I told them about it and they were sorry, and gave the money back."

5. "We finished rebuilding the wall in just fifty-two days. Our enemies got scared, as they knew God must be with us. If God was with us they were afraid things might go badly for them."

6. "Later on, everyone came back to Jerusalem from Babylon. Ezra read the Bible to them for hours. The Levites sang to God and thanked him for forgiving our sins and saving us from our enemies. The Levites, the other leaders and all the people promised to obey God."

7. "I worked to make sure that God was worshiped properly at the *temple*, so that people were doing what God wanted, and not just anything. I also discovered that some men had disobeyed God by marrying women from other countries, who didn't love God. This made me upset and angry because I knew it would lead the men to stop loving God as well.""

LEARNING FROM NEHEMIAH

1. God blessed Nehemiah by making the king decide to let him go home to Israel for a while. Then God blessed his people by warning them that others wanted to attack, and helped them to build the city wall of Jerusalem very quickly. We need God's help and protection, too – not from people who don't want us to build a wall, but from people who want us to disobey God (See overview paragraphs 1, 3 and 5).

    Bible references: Nehemiah 2:6–8, 6:16; Proverbs 1:10; 1 Peter 4:4.

    Questions: Do you find it hard to be kind when other people are mean? Do you find it hard to obey your parents or teachers when people around you are being disobedient? Ask God to protect the way you think, so that you still want to obey him.

2. God cares about people who can't help or defend themselves, and people who are treated badly. He wants us to care about them, too. Ask God to help you be fair with people, and not be like the rich people in Nehemiah's day who were unfair to the poor (See overview paragraph 4).

    Bible references: Nehemiah 5:9-12; Deuteronomy 10:18; James 1:27.

    Question: Can you think of people who really need your help? Talk to a grown-up about people who don't have enough food or are treated badly. Pray for them, and talk about how you could help them.

3. After the Jews had said a big thank you to God for saving them from their enemies and forgiving their sins, they promised to obey God. One of the ways that we know God has forgiven our sins is if we want to obey God. Ask God to help you with that (See overview paragraph 6).

    Bible references: Nehemiah 10:28-29; 2 John 6.

    Question: Think of all the things that God has done for you. (for example, making you, giving you a place to live, food to eat, and being healthy) Has he given you forgiveness for your sins? What would you like to do for God?

SALVATION THREAD

Long before the exile, God promised to send a Savior who would be born in Bethlehem. So when God brought his people back from Babylon, he wasn't just keeping his covenant with them, he was also keeping alive the hope of a Savior.

If God's people were kept in Babylon, or destroyed in war, there could be no Savior. But God always keeps his promises. So he took them home and kept them safe there.

Key Verse: "And because the gracious hand of my God was upon me, the king granted my requests" (Nehemiah 2:8).

The book of
ESTHER

ESTHER

God's good plans for his people cannot be beaten

INTRODUCTION

- God's name is not mentioned in the book of Esther, but it tells us amazing things about God! It took place while a lot of God's people were still in *exile*, and Xerxes was king. We don't know who wrote the book. It was probably a Jew, and may have been Mordecai, who is in the story.

- The main events of this book were some time between 485 and 464 B.C.

OVERVIEW

1. "King Xerxes had a big feast for many important people. When he was drunk he told his wife, Vashti, to come to him so he could show her off to his guests because she was good-looking. She said no. Xerxes got so angry he sent her away and stopped her from being queen."

2. "The king decided to choose another woman to be his wife and queen. He looked at many women to see who he liked. Esther was chosen, even though she was really a Jew and did not belong in that country."

3. "Esther's uncle Mordecai found out that some people were trying to kill the king, so he told Esther who warned the king, and Xerxes was saved."

4. "The king then made a man called Haman so important that everyone bowed to him, but Mordecai said he would not bow to him. This made Haman so angry that he decided to kill all Mordecai's people, the Jews. He got the king to sign a law to do this. Esther was afraid to speak to the king, who sometimes killed just for annoying him. But Mordecai said she needed to brave and see the king, so she did.

5. "Then she invited Xerxes and Haman to come to a feast. At the feast, Esther told Xerxes that she was a Jew, and begged him to save her people. She said it was Haman's idea to have them killed. Because the king liked Esther, he had Haman killed. He encouraged the Jews to fight back when people went to kill them. The Jews defeated their enemies, who were now scared because the Jews had the king's support."

6. "The Jews decided that every year they would remember those days when they were saved from their enemies, and Mordecai became the second most important person, behind only the king."

LEARNING FROM ESTHER

1. There is no point going against God – sooner or later you will lose because he is in charge of everything. Haman was going against God by trying to kill God's people. We are going against God if we deliberately disobey him or are nasty to people because they believe in him (See overview paragraphs 4–5).

   Bible references: Esther 8:17; Psalm 2:1-2, 4-5; 2 Timothy 4:14-15.

   Questions: How did God stop Haman killing all the Jews? Why did Haman think he could get away with going against God by killing the Jews?

2. However bad things are, or however much trouble we are in, it is never so bad that God cannot save us. The Jews were all just about to get killed, but God protected them. We should ask God to protect us from the Devil, who wants us to disobey God and not to love him (See overview paragraphs 5–6).

   Bible references: Esther 9:20-22; Matthew 6:13; Romans 8:31, 35-39.

   Question: Do you realize that God can do anything? Do you pray for big things to happen, or just small things? Ask God for some big things, such as healing from sickness, safety in danger, or the biggest thing: forgiveness of sins.

3. God is in charge of everything, but we are still responsible for what we do. Mordecai told Esther to speak with Xerxes to stop the Jews being killed. He told her that the Jews would be saved some other way if she wouldn't do it, but she would suffer. He said God had her in a great time and place to do a good work and she should do it (See overview paragraph 4).

   Bible references: Esther 4:14; Matthew 26:24; Acts 3:23.

   Question: Do you sometimes make excuses to your teacher or parents, or even in your own head, when you do bad things? Perhaps you sometimes think that when you have been bad it is not really your fault? Remember that God says it is our fault when we sin, but that he loves to forgive us for our sins.

SALVATION THREAD

If Haman got what he wanted, all the Jews would have been killed – not just those in Babylon but also those who went home to Israel. This was another time when it looked like God's promise of a Messiah (Jesus) would not come true because all God's people, the Jews, might be killed.

Again, God did not let that happen, but he protected his people using Mordecai, Esther and even the wicked King Xerxes himself. Mordecai was thinking about this in chapter 4, verse 14; he was trying to persuade the scared Queen Esther to go and see the king, and he said, "… who knows but that you have come to royal position for such a time as this?"

Matthew chapter 1 gives a list of people from Abraham through to Jesus. If Haman had been successful, the list would end at verse 12 because the Jews would have been wiped out. No more Jews, no Jesus. But God did not let that happen, because he always keeps his promises.

Key Verse: "… Queen Esther answered, 'If I have found favor with you, O king, and if it pleases your majesty, grant me my life … And spare my people …" (Esther 7:3).

POETRY AND WISDOM

The book of
JOB

JOB

Perseverance in suffering

INTRODUCTION

- Imagine the worst things that could happen to you. What if they came true? The worst things coming true is what happened to Job. We don't know much about him except that God says in the book of Ezekiel that he was a very good man. James, who wrote in the New Testament, said Job is a good example of loving God even when life is hard.

- Job may have lived shortly before and after 2000 B.C.

OVERVIEW

1. "There was once a great man called Job who loved God. He had ten children and was very rich."

2. "Satan said to God that Job only loved God because Job had lots of things, a big family and was healthy. God knew that was not true, and allowed Satan to do horrible things to Job to prove that Job would always love God, no matter what happened. Everything Job had was stolen, his children died, he became sick and was in a lot of pain all the time. Four of his friends came to try and make him feel better."

3. "Job then said he wished he had never been born because his life was so horrible. He didn't think he had done anything wrong but that God was hurting him and there was nothing he could do about it. But he didn't say that God was wrong."

4. "Three of his friends said everything bad that happens to people is God punishing them, so Job and his children must have done something very bad. They told Job to say sorry for what he had done."

5. "Job would not agree that he was being punished and after a while his friends gave up saying those things. Then the fourth friend said the other three were unhelpful and that Job thought too much about how good he was and not enough about God."

6. "God spoke to Job and said 'I made everything, I know how everything works and what is best. You don't know those things so why are you arguing with me?' He was angry with Job's friends – they were wrong to say that God was punishing Job. They thought they understood God, but did not."

7. "After this Job was healed from his diseases, had ten more children and God gave him lots of things. Job's life was even better after his great suffering than it was before."

LEARNING FROM JOB

1. We don't understand everything but God does. That's okay. Trust God that he knows best (See overview paragraph 6).

    Bible references: Job 1:22; 2:10; Isaiah 55:7-9; Philippians 4:6-7.

    Questions: Do you know as much as your parents about driving a car or cooking? Do you trust them to do those things without them telling you how they do it? How much more should we trust what God does in our lives?

2. Bad things happen for lots of different reasons. Because something bad happens to someone, does not mean they did something wrong or they are being punished (See overview paragraphs 4 and 6).

    Bible references: Job 42:7; John 9:1-3; Luke 13:4; 2 Corinthians 11:23-27.

    Questions: Can you think of someone who never did anything wrong, but horrible things happened to him? Read 2 Corinthians 11:23–27. Paul lists some horrible things that happened to him. Were any of those a punishment from God?

3. It is easy to love God when everything is nice. God wants us to love him properly, and that means even when we are sick or don't have anything or are sad (See overview paragraphs 2–3).

    Bible references: Job 1:9–2:10; 2 Corinthians 1:8-11; 5:7; 1 Peter 1:7-8.

    Question: How can you show God you love him even when you are sad?

SALVATION THREAD

If we have repented of our sins to God then he has forgiven us and we are saved. But, we are not yet in *heaven*! We must wait patiently, with *faith*, for that amazing day when we will go to be with God forever. Satan tried to make Job lose his *faith* by telling him that all the bad things happening to him were his own fault. But Job knew that he had not rebelled against God, and was still faithful to God.

Satan still tells that lie to God's people because he wants them to think they won't go to heaven and they can't trust God.

When *Satan* accuses us of *sin* we can admit that we are sinners, but we can also know that because Jesus has died to pay the price for our *sin* we are forgiven. Our sins are taken away and no-one can accuse us any more! (Isaiah 50:9; Revelation 12:10-11).

Key Verse: "As you know, we consider blessed those who have persevered. You have heard of Job's perseverance and have seen what the Lord finally brought about. The Lord is full of compassion and *mercy*" (James 5:11).

The book of
PSALMS

PSALM 69

A desperate man's call to his Savior

A psalm is a song, and the book of Psalms is a songbook. The psalms are about different things, and by different people. In this book we will look at two psalms, rather than try to understand all at once. Below is a shortened version of Psalm 69.[25]

INTRODUCTION

- Have you ever felt like you were drowning? King David, who probably wrote this psalm, was having such a horrible time that he could hardly keep going any more – it was like he was drowning.

- Psalm 69 was probably written some time between 1125 and 1050 B.C.

OVERVIEW

1. "Save me, O God! I am in deep water and the waves are about to drown me. I am worn out from calling for help, and my throat is aching. I have strained my eyes, looking for your help. I have more enemies than hairs on my head, and they have no reason to hate me. They tell lies against me; they are strong and want to kill me."

2. "My sins, O God, are not hidden from you; you know how foolish I have been. Don't let me bring shame on those who trust in you, Sovereign LORD Almighty! It is for your sake that I have been insulted and that I am covered with shame."

3. "I love the temple where we worship you; the insults people throw at you, fall on me. I humble myself by fasting, and people insult me; I dress myself in clothes of mourning, and they laugh at me."

4. "But as for me, I will pray to you, LORD; answer me because of your great love, because you keep your promise to save. Save me from sinking in the mud; keep me safe from my enemies, safe from the deep water."

5. "Answer me, LORD, in the goodness of your constant love – turn to me! Don't hide yourself from your servant; I am in great trouble, answer me now! Come to me and save me; rescue me from my enemies. Punish them severely!"

6. "God, may your *salvation* protect me! I will praise the great God with a song and thankfulness. This will please the LORD more than sacrifices. When those who are badly treated see my trust in God who saves me, they will be glad; those who worship God will be encouraged. The LORD listens to those in need."

---

25. Part or all of the following verses have been left out: 1, 4, 6, 8, 12, 15, 19-27.

7. "Praise God, O *heaven* and earth, seas and all creatures in them. He will save Jerusalem and rebuild the towns of Judah. Those who love God will live there. God, you are awesome and you give power and strength to your people. May God be praised!"

LEARNING FROM PSALM 69

1. When we are in trouble we should turn to God. The trouble can be because of our sin, or people being mean to us, or other bad things that are happening. We should always go to God (See overview paragraphs 1–5, 7).

   Bible references: Psalm 69:1, 3, 5; 2 Chronicles 25:15; Hebrews 13:6.

   Questions: It is only God who always hears our cries for help. Do you call to him to help you fight against *sin*, or only when you need help with other things?

2. God looks after his people and will bless them, no matter how bad things might be. We need to be patient and wait for God's help. This help can be when God gets us out of our difficult times in our life, or when he helps us trust him through those difficult times (See overview paragraphs 4–5).

   Bible references: Psalm 69:10, 17; Isaiah 8:17, 35:4; James 5:7-8.

   Question: Do you find it hard when God doesn't say "yes" to a prayer straight away? God always blesses his people, even when it doesn't feel good, and even when he doesn't say "yes" to what we want.

3. God always deserves our praise and our thanks, because of who he is, what he has done and what he is still doing (See overview paragraph 2).

   Bible references: Psalm 69:30-31, 34-35; Psalm 150; Luke 1:68-71.

   Questions: Why do you think God deserves your praise and thanks? What has he done for you that you can thank him for?

SALVATION THREAD

This psalm is mentioned in the New Testament more often than any other psalm except Psalm 22. A lot of this psalm is a picture of what happened in Jesus' life. For example:

• Psalm 69:4 / John 15:25: The Psalmist, and Jesus, were hated without good reason.

• Psalm 69:9 / John 2:17: When Jesus cleared the temple of people who were turning it into a market, his disciples remembered this verse by the psalmist.

• Psalm 69:21 / Matthew 27:48: When Jesus was about to be crucified, he was given the same sharp drink that the psalmist talks about.

• Psalm 69:8 / John 7:5: Jesus was rejected by his own people, even his own brothers.

The psalmist knows that he needs saving by God, and we must remember that it is only God who can save us from our biggest enemy: our own sin (v. 13).

The psalmist also knew that just making sacrifices and doing all the right things wouldn't please God – what God wants is people who truly thank, praise and worship him (v. 31).

Key Verse: "But I pray to you, LORD, in the time of your favor; in your great love, O God, answer me with your sure *salvation*" (Psalm 69:13).

PSALM 103

Me, you, everyone: praise the Lord!

INTRODUCTION

- Imagine being so full of joy about our wonderful God that you can't help singing about him! David felt like that when he wrote this psalm. He wrote it in Hebrew, and each line begins with a different letter of the Hebrew alphabet.

- Psalm 103 was probably written some time between 1125 and 1050 B.C.

OVERVIEW

1. "I will praise the LORD, and praise his name, from the bottom of my heart. May I never forget the good things he does for me. He forgives all my sins and heals all my diseases. He saves me, and covers me with love and mercy. He fills my life with good things. I feel young, strong, and full of energy because of God. I feel like an eagle soaring so high!"

2. "The LORD gives righteousness and justice to all who are treated unfairly."

3. "God showed Moses what God is like, and did amazing things for Israel. The LORD is full of love and mercy and does not get angry easily or quickly. He does not hold grudges. We deserve to be treated very badly because of all our sin, but God doesn't do that."

4. "God's love keeps going, it never stops. It's as tall as the sky for those who respect and love God. He has removed our sins as far from us as the east is from the west. The LORD is like a father to his children, gentle and kind to those who greatly respect him. For he knows how weak we are, that we are nothing compared to him. Our lives are so short. The wind blows, and we are gone – as though we had never been here. But the love of the LORD remains forever with those who respect him. God is faithful to all those who obey him, cleaning them from their sin and keeping all of his promises."

5. "The LORD has made the sky and the whole universe to be like a throne. From there he rules over everything."

6. "Praise the LORD, you angels, you mighty ones who carry out his plans, listening for each of his commands. Yes, praise the LORD, you armies of angels who serve him and do his will! Praise the LORD, everything he has created, everything in all his kingdom. Let me praise the LORD from the bottom of my heart."[26]

---

26. Paraphrase based on the New Living Translation.

LEARNING FROM PSALM 103

1. David reminded himself that God did many good things for him. He was most thankful that God forgave his sins and the sins of God's people. If God has forgiven your sins, every part of you should be saying, "Thank you!" (See overview paragraphs 1 and 4).

   Bible references: Psalm 103:2-5, 10-12, 17-18; Micah 7:18-19; Ephesians 2:4-5.

   Questions: What good things did God do for David? Can you think of good things God has done for you? Make a list and keep it in your Bible to remind you.

2. God deserves our praise because of who he is and what he is like, and not just because of what he does. King David said that God is holy (this means perfect), and he is just (which means he is always fair). God is like a perfect Dad – loving and patient. Also, God rules over everything (See overview paragraphs 1–2, 4–5).

   Bible references: Psalm 103:1, 6-9, 13, 19; Daniel 2:20; Revelation 7:12.

   Questions: Write down all the words you can think of to describe God. What made you think of those words?

3. When God forgives sins, they are completely gone, forever (See overview paragraphs 1, 3–4).

   Bible references: Psalm 103:12; Isaiah 43:25; Romans 8:1-2.

   Question: What would it feel like if your parents forgave you for something wrong you did, but then reminded you of your sin every day? Do you think God would do that?

SALVATION THREAD

"Praise the LORD, everything he has created, everything in all his kingdom" (Psalm 103:22, NLT).

David gave a picture of the creation singing to God – not just people, but everything God has made. He didn't know it then, but that fits with a picture that we have of *heaven* from the book of Revelation, written over 1,000 years later: "Then I heard every creature in *heaven* and on earth and under the earth and on the sea, and all that is in them, singing: 'To him who sits on the throne and to the Lamb be praise and honor and *glory* and power, for ever and ever!'" (Revelation 5:13).

That is because God is going to make all of creation new again, to be ruled over by God's people (Romans 8:21-22). God deserved praise from all of creation back in David's time, and he deserves it now. One day, when Jesus comes again it really will feel like every animal, tree, mountain, sea and flower is praising God because everything will be perfect.

Key Verse: "Let all that I am praise the LORD; with my whole heart, I will praise his *holy* name" (Psalm 103:1, NLT).

The book of
PROVERBS

PROVERBS

God helps us to be wise

INTRODUCTION

- Proverbs is full of good advice about how to live wisely. That shouldn't surprise you because it was put together, and mostly written, by Solomon who was made very smart by God. Doing smart things does not make us Christians – God does that for us without us deserving it. But Christians need to be careful to avoid sin and please God – that is living wisely. Proverbs was written as poetry. It doesn't rhyme, but there are many word pictures to help us understand what was meant.

- Proverbs was probably written some time between 960 and 930 B.C.

OVERVIEW

1. "Listen to what your parents teach you; listen to wisdom. Don't give in to people who want you to sin with them; stay away from them. Their sins will come back to hurt them."

2. "If you are foolish you get angry very easily, but if you are wise you won't try to get your own back when people are nasty to you."

3. "God gives wisdom, which will save you from falling into sin; trust in God, who sees what you do and think. He hates it when people lie; liars think they are better than they are, and cause arguments."

4. "Foolishness is loud but doesn't know anything."

5. "A good parent will discipline their child. Good discipline helps the child to remember what God says and to obey God always."

6. "Being poor but having love and loving God, is better than being rich with hate around you. You shouldn't spend loads of time trying to get rich."

7. "God hates unfairness and dishonesty. Look after the poor, and stand up for people who can't stand up for themselves."

8. "People make many plans, but it is up to God what happens."

9. "Relying on a person you can't trust is like having toothache."

10. "If your enemy is hungry, give him something to eat."

11. "Everything God says is perfect, and he is a shield for people who go to him for protection. Don't add anything to what God says."

12. "Who can find a wife who is a very good person? She is way more precious than jewels; she looks after her family and does many other good things. Her husband has everything he needs and he praises her."

LEARNING FROM PROVERBS

1. Ask God for wisdom. Only God can teach us how to follow and obey him. Only he can give us wisdom. Because wisdom is so important, we should always want to know more about what God says (See overview paragraphs 1, 3 and 5).

   Bible references: Proverbs 1:2, 7; 1 Kings 3:5, 9-12; Ephesians 1:17; James 1:5.

   Questions: Do you always know what is the best thing to do to please God? Who do you think would know best what pleases God?

2. There are some things – sinful behaviors – that God hates and we should hate them too. (See overview paragraphs 3 and 6).

   Bible references: Proverbs 6:16-19; 11:1; Psalm 97:10; Matthew 23:23; Colossians 3:5.

   Question: What are some of the things that God hates? Do you hate them? If so, what are you doing to get rid of them from your life?

3. God is in charge of everything, knows everything, and his Word is perfect, so he is the only one we can trust totally and believe (See overview paragraphs 3, 7–8)

   Bible references: Proverbs 16:9; 19:21; 30:5; 2 Samuel 7:28; Psalm 19:7; Titus 1:9.

   Question: Think of what God has said in the Bible. Can you believe what he says?

SALVATION THREAD

Some of the Proverbs are written as if wisdom is a person: "Blessed is the man who listens to me, watching daily at my doors, waiting at my doorway. For whoever finds me finds life and receives favor from the LORD. But whoever fails to find me harms himself; all who hate me love death" (Proverbs 8: 34-36).

In the New Testament, there is only one person described as being like that: Jesus. Paul the apostle wrote, "It is because of [God] that you are in Christ Jesus, who has become for us wisdom from God – that is, our righteousness, holiness and redemption" (1 Corinthians 1:30).

If we don't have wisdom then we don't have life with God, and if we don't have Jesus then we don't have life with God. So, we can say that wisdom is a picture of Jesus.

Key Verse: "The fear of the LORD is the beginning of knowledge, but fools despise wisdom and discipline" (Proverbs 1:7).

The book of
ECCLESIASTES

ECCLESIASTES

What am I doing here?

INTRODUCTION

- What is the point of life? What should we be doing? Even wise King Solomon, who probably wrote Ecclesiastes, was confused about it for a long time. This book shows him asking good questions about life, and looking for purpose and meaning. He was honest in what he wrote about things in life that seemed hard and unfair.

- Ecclesiastes was written some time after 1000 B.C.

OVERVIEW

1. "Everything is meaningless – it keeps going on as always. Chasing after wisdom is meaningless. Everyone gets forgotten. Chasing after fun is meaningless, like chasing the wind. So is going after money, keeping busy or spending all your time working. This is depressing. All you can do is eat, drink and be happy with that. This is how God designed it. There is a right time for doing lots of different things. I don't know what happens when you die."

2. "Lots of people get treated badly and have no help. Most things people do are just because they want more things than others. It is good to have friends. Respect God and be careful about what you say. Just dreaming and talking about things is meaningless."

3. "You are born, you live and you die. You can't get enough money or things and you can't take things with you when you die. Wisdom is a good thing. It is better than foolishness but most people don't listen to it. Foolishness destroys wisdom and it destroys the fool in the end."

4. "Obey your rulers otherwise it will be bad for you. Good people getting bad things and bad people getting good things makes no sense, so just enjoy your meaningless life as long as God lets you live."

5. "There is no way to understand wisdom. Everyone dies so what is the point of it all? Work hard and don't try to work out what God is doing. Do what you want but remember God will pay you back for all of it."

6. "Turn to God while you are young, before what happens in life distracts you, and before it is too late. The words of the wise are all given by God."

7. "In the end, this is what matters: respect God greatly and obey him, because God will judge all the good and bad things that are done."

LEARNING FROM ECCLESIASTES

1. When people realize that everyone dies, that nothing lasts forever, and that bad things happen, they sometimes get sad and don't understand why life is like that. It can feel like there's no point to it all (See overview paragraphs 1–5).

    Bible references: Ecclesiastes 9:9; 1 Timothy 6:17; Ephesians 2:12.

    Question: What are some of the wrong ideas about life that people have?

2. Lots of people have good ideas or want to do good things, but mainly they like to talk about it. That is no use – we have to do the good things, not just talk about it! (See overview paragraph 2).

    Bible references: Ecclesiastes 3:12; 5:4-5; 1 Samuel 2:3; Ephesians 2:10.

    Questions: What ideas do you have about how you can do good things? How can you make sure they happen?

3. Many people never learn wisdom from God. Others learn it the hard way like the writer of Ecclesiastes, who wasted a lot of time and effort trying to find meaning through work, fun or money. With Ecclesiastes, God is giving us an opportunity to find important wisdom right away – without having to make lots of bad choices first like Solomon did. Ecclesiastes teaches that respecting and obeying God should be our focus – that is living wisely (See overview paragraph 7).

    Bible references: Ecclesiastes 12:1, 13; Proverbs 2:16; James 3:17.

    Question: What did Solomon do to try and find happiness and meaning? Can you think of wise advice or instructions you have been given that you ignored and had to learn wisdom the hard way? (For example, maybe your parents warned you about jumping off something high, or wandering off on your own?).

SALVATION THREAD

We might want to understand and know everything, but we can't. Only God can. Sometimes if we try to know everything we end up losing sight of the simple things that we need to know.

That happened to the writer of Ecclesiastes for a while. He thought he could work out for himself what life was all about, but the harder he looked the more it all seemed to be "meaningless".[27] He tried everything he could until finally, when he realized he couldn't make sense of life, he saw the answer to everything: "Fear God and keep his commandments, for this is the whole duty of man."[28] God, he recognized, had all the answers. We should look to God and not ourselves to understand what life is all about.[29]

Key Verse: "Fear God and keep his commandments, for this is the whole duty of man" (Ecclesiastes 12:13).

---

27. Ecclesiastes 1:2 & 12:8.
28. Ecclesiastes 12:13.
29. Ecclesiastes 12:12-13.

The book of
SONG OF SONGS

SONG OF SONGS

The greatest love poem ever written

INTRODUCTION

- God put a love poem in the middle of the Bible! It tells the story of a man and woman in love. They dream of being together and, near the end of the book, are married. It is a long poem split into sections. Sometimes the woman speaks, sometimes the man, and sometimes their friends. "Song of Songs" is a way of calling the poem great. It's not just any old song – it's the greatest, it's the song of songs!

- Song of Songs was probably written some time between 960 and 930 B.C.

OVERVIEW

1. Woman: I want him to kiss me – his love is wonderful.

2. Friends: You and your love are lovely.

3. Man: Where are you my love? You are a most beautiful woman.

4. Woman: And you are precious to me and so handsome. I am like a rose and the man who loves me is like an apple tree that protects me and provides sweet fruit. But do not love in the special way until the proper time.

5. Man: Let me see you and hear you and let nothing spoil our love.

6. Woman: My lover is mine and I am his. I missed him so much and looked for him until I found him.

7. Man: How beautiful you are, my darling! I love your face. You are all that is lovely and you have my heart.

8. Friends: Enjoy each other you lovers!

9. Woman: I was in bed when my lover came to my door. I didn't get up soon enough. When I did he was gone and now I really want to see him. My friends, if you find him tell him I am totally in love with him.

10. Friends: Why? How is he better than other men? And where did he go?

11. Woman: My lover, my friend is very handsome, impressive and lovely. I am his and he is mine.

12. Man: You are so beautiful; I can hardly cope with it when you look at me!

13. Friends: Who is this handsome person arriving? Come back so that we can look at you!

14. Man: Your graceful legs are like jewels – precious and gorgeous and perfect. Your whole body is beautiful and I want to enjoy it.

15. Woman: I want you to enjoy my body. I belong to you and you want me. I want everyone to see that I love you. Love me forever. But do not love in the special way

until the proper time. True love cannot be taken away; it is intense and worth more than any treasure. I am ready for marriage.

16. Man: Let me hear your voice!

17. Woman: Come away, my lover. Be with me and show me how wonderful you are.

LEARNING FROM SONG OF SONGS

1. God's plan for marriage is that a husband and wife will enjoy each other and will want to be together as much as possible (See overview paragraphs 1-17).

   Bible references: Song of Songs 1:1, 4; Proverbs 5:18; Ephesians 5:28-29.

   Question: Who do you like spending time with? If you get married, God wants you to be happy with that person; to spend lots of time with them.

2. When a man and a woman get married it is like they are joined together to become one person. When we become a *Christian* we are joined together with Jesus and he will love us and stay with us forever (See overview paragraphs 6 and 15).

   Bible reference: Song of Songs 8:6-7; Hosea 2:19; Ephesians 5:31-32.

   Question: What would it be like if you were with your best friends all the time? A good marriage is even better than that. And a right relationship with God is even better than a good marriage.

3. The love that Song of Songs talks about is for a husband and wife. The love of a husband and wife is a picture in the Bible of the love between Jesus and the Church. Jesus loved his people so much that he was willing to suffer and die so that we could be saved from sin. He still loves us and wants to help us enjoy God more (See overview paragraph 15).

   Bible reference: Song of Songs 8:7; Isaiah 62:4-5; Ephesians 5:25-27.

   Question: What do you think marriage would be like if the husband loved the wife as much as Jesus loves his people?

SALVATION THREAD

Song of Songs is one of only two books in the Bible that do not mention God by name – the other is Esther. But God speaks to us through the book of Esther and he speaks to us through Solomon's Song of Songs.

God invented marriage to be a wonderful picture of the relationship between Jesus Christ and the Church – God's people. The great love of Jesus for his people, doing everything for them to make them perfect, loving them, giving himself up for them, taking them to God as a glorious gift … God wanted to show us all of that through the marriage of a man and a woman.

Through sin, that picture was spoiled. There is so much unhappiness, and so many marriages where it's hard to see a good picture of love, but here God gives us a picture of how amazing marriage is designed to be. God designed it to be enjoyable, useful, and to make a husband and wife full of joy … which is also how God designed our relationship with Him.

Key Verses: "… he is altogether lovely. This is my lover, this my friend …" (Song of Songs 5:16).

"Husbands, love your wives, just as Christ loved the church and gave himself up for her …" (Ephesians 5:25).

MAJOR PROPHETS

The book of

ISAIAH

ISAIAH

Immanuel, God with us

INTRODUCTION

- Isaiah was a prophet to Judah – a country in trouble. They went through four kings during Isaiah's time and God sent other prophets: Amos, Hosea, and Micah. God told Judah's people through Isaiah that they would be taken away from their homes. But his message was also about how God would save his people. Several of those prophecies were fulfilled by Jesus.

- Isaiah was a prophet from about 740 to 680 B.C.

OVERVIEW

1. "This is the vision from God to the *prophet* Isaiah."

2. "God will punish evil: the proud, those who reject God, the unjust and the cruel. Most people have rejected God but he will make sure it is not everyone. Peace will come through God but people must trust him. He keeps telling people about himself and warns them to obey him but they keep ignoring him."

3. "In the end, God's people will have nothing but happiness, but there will be suffering first. God will use one country to punish another country."

4. "One day, the King of Assyria attacked Judah and was going to attack the capital city Jerusalem. But God wouldn't let him defeat God's people, and instead caused his army to be wiped out. King Hezekiah of Judah then became ill and was about to die but God answered his prayer to be made better. However, Hezekiah then started showing off his treasures to people from Babylon, and Isaiah gave a message from God that all the treasure would be lost and God's people taken away from their country."

5. "What God says lasts forever, and God will show that he is the only true God."

6. "When God punishes his people, it is because he wants them to *repent*. In the end God will use the one he sends – the *Messiah* – to bring all of his people back to him. God's people have been saved by him and do not need to be afraid of anything. They will be blessed by him."

7. "God's people will go all over the world to tell people about him, bringing all of God's people to him."

LEARNING FROM ISAIAH

1. A good relationship with God is so important that God sometimes needs to punish his people when they allow *sin* to get in the way of that relationship. He wants to remind them that they need him, like children sometimes need to be reminded how much they need their parents (See overview paragraph 6).

    Bible references: Isaiah 9:13-14; Hebrews 12:5-11.

    Questions: What do you think about when you are being punished? That it's not fair? That other people are worse than you? Or that you need to talk to God about it?

2. God hates pride. It turns us away from him (See overview paragraphs 2 and 4).

    Bible references: Isaiah 2:11, 37:23; Proverbs 8:13; 16:18.

    Questions: Do you sometimes feel like you don't need God? Why?

3. If we belong to God then we never need to be afraid because he will always keep us – even though we are still sinful (See overview paragraphs 2, 3 and 6).

    Bible references: Isaiah 41:13-14, 43:1; Psalm 23:4; Romans 8:1.

    Questions: When are you tempted to think that maybe God doesn't love you anymore? When you're sad? When you've been sinful?

SALVATION THREAD

"Therefore the Lord himself will give you a sign: The virgin will be with child and will give birth to a son, and will call him Immanuel" (Isaiah 7:14).

"… an angel of the Lord appeared to him in a dream and said, 'Joseph son of David, do not be afraid to take Mary home as your wife, because what is conceived in her is from the Holy Spirit. She will give birth to a son, and you are to give him the name Jesus, because he will save his people from their sins.' All this took place to fulfill what the Lord had said through the *prophet*: 'The virgin will be with child and will give birth to a son, and they will call him Immanuel – which means, "God with us"'" (Matthew 1:20–23).

Isaiah is mentioned twenty times in the New Testament because so many of his prophecies are about Jesus, including this one from Matthew chapter one. It's amazing to think that Isaiah's prophecies, written 700 years before Jesus was born, came true! They are more examples of how God always keeps his promises, his Word is true, and therefore God can always be trusted.

Key Verse: "Let the wicked forsake his way and the evil man his thoughts. Let him turn to the Lord, and he will have mercy on him, and to our God, for he will freely pardon" (Isaiah 55:7).

The book of

JEREMIAH

JEREMIAH

God warns, God punishes and God saves

INTRODUCTION

- Jeremiah is the longest book in the Bible. It contains the words of the prophet Jeremiah, given to him by God and written down by Jeremiah's secretary and friend, Baruch. The name "Jeremiah" means, "the Lord throws". Jeremiah and the nation of Israel were thrown into a terrible time in their history. The book was written as if it was Jeremiah speaking.

- Jeremiah was a prophet from about 627 to 585 B.C.

OVERVIEW

1. "The word of God came to me and said, 'I choose you to be a prophet, and I will be with you always and tell you everything you need to say.'"

2. "God asked Israel: 'Why are you rejecting me, even though I have done so many good things for you? Why are you worshiping false gods, which do nothing for you because they're not real?'"

3. "'Many times I sent prophets to remind you to repent, but you did not. I punished you to remind you to repent, but you did not.'"

4. "'You are nasty to poor people and do other bad things, but then you worship at the temple because you think that makes everything OK. It doesn't. If you obey me I will bless you, but if you keep rejecting me, I will punish you badly. You will be attacked, many people will die, and many others will be taken away from your country. Don't believe the false prophets who say everything will be fine – they are lying.'"

5. "'However, one day I will bring you back to your own country. I will forgive your sins and show my glory to everyone because of everything I do for you. All the promises to bless you that I made, and am making now, will come true.'"

6. "Many of the people hated Jeremiah for telling them God would punish them if they didn't repent. They said bad things to Jeremiah. They beat him and put him in prison; some even tried to kill him. This made Jeremiah very sad, but he wouldn't stop telling people what God said."

7. "Later, Babylon attacked Israel and all the bad things happened just as God told Jeremiah they would. God also told Jeremiah about punishments for other countries that said no to God, and said he would forgive people if they were truly sorry. Babylon would never be sorry and they will be punished forever."

LEARNING FROM JEREMIAH

1. God is very patient, but he will not put up with sin forever. He will punish it in the end if people do not ask for forgiveness (See overview paragraphs 3–4).

   Bible references: Jeremiah 15:7; Ezekiel 7:7-8; 2 Peter 3:9.

   Questions: Do you sometimes think that doing bad things is okay if you don't get punished for it?

2. God showed the *Israelites* his love by telling them many times that they needed to be sorry for their sins and come back to him. God does the same thing for us through what we read about sin and forgiveness in the Bible (See overview paragraphs 4, 6–7).

   Bible references: Jeremiah 7:25; Matthew 21:33-36; Hebrews 12:10-11.

   Question: Do you think about what you should do – or only about what you want? Have you listened to what God says about *sin* and forgiveness?

3. God always does as he says. He keeps his promises. So when he warns us about bad things, we need to take him seriously. And when he says that good will happen, we can be happy because we know it's true. Thank God that he keeps his promises (See overview paragraphs 5 and 7).

   Bible references: Jeremiah 33:20-21; Joshua 21:45; 2 Corinthians 1:20.

   Questions: Can you remember some of the promises God has made? How has he kept those promises? (e.g. Genesis 9:11; 15:4 and 21:1; Luke 2:26-29; Acts 2:29-32).

SALVATION THREAD

"The days are coming," declares the LORD, "when I will raise up to David a righteous Branch, a King who will reign wisely and do what is just and right in the land. In his days Judah will be saved and Israel will live in safety. This is the name by which he will be called: The LORD Our Righteousness" (Jeremiah 23: 5-6).

"… Christ Jesus, who has become for us wisdom from God – that is, our *righteousness*, holiness and redemption" (1 Corinthians 1:30).

Jesus was from the family of David (Matthew 1:1), he is our King (John 18:37), and he is our *righteousness* if we are Christians.

To be *righteous* means to do all things right and be totally without sin. Jesus never sinned, there is no sin in him, and he covers his people with his *righteousness* (Romans 4:24) like a coat (Galatians 3:27). That means that when God looks at his people, he doesn't see *sin* or badness, he sees the *righteousness* that Jesus has given to us. Because Jesus gives his people his *righteousness*, we can have a relationship with God and be with him forever.

God also talked about the new *covenant* that he will make with his people. In Jeremiah 31:31-34 (also written in Hebrews 8:8-12), God said that he will have a one-on-one relationship with all his people, unlike in the Old Testament when they knew God from stories, their Bible, and through the priests.

Key Verse: "… let him who boasts, boast about this: that he understands and knows me, that I am the LORD, who exercises kindness, justice and *righteousness* on earth, for in these I delight" (Jeremiah 9:24).

The book of
LAMENTATIONS

LAMENTATIONS

Oh no, how could this happen?!

INTRODUCTION

- Imagine that you had to warn people about a disaster, and then it happened because they ignored you. This is what happened to Jeremiah. The Babylonians invaded Judah. The book is like one big, "Argh, oh no!" when that happened, in the style of a poem, using word pictures.

- Lamentations was written some time between 587 and 516 B.C.

OVERVIEW

1. "The city lies empty, that was once so full of people. It is like a crying widow with no-one to comfort her because all her friends have become her enemies. Judah's many sins have ruined her and she remembers how wonderful life used to be. All her people groan as they search for bread, trying to keep themselves alive. My sins have come down on my head like a great weight – *The LORD is righteous, yet I rebelled against his command.*"[30]

2. "God has trampled the country like people trample grapes to make wine. This is why I am crying. My enemies laugh and are happy at my misery; God, I hope you will punish them for their sins as you have punished me for mine. God has covered his people with the cloud of his anger, torn down their buildings and reduced them to shame. He has poured out his terrible anger like fire and taken away his right hand of protection."

3. "*My heart is poured out on the ground because my people are destroyed.*[31] Even children die in their mother's arms. *Your wound is as deep as the sea. Who can heal you? ...The visions of your prophets were false and worthless*"[32] – they did not show you your sin, so that you could repent and be saved."

4. "I have seen God's terrible punishments, but I remember this and it gives me hope: Because of the LORD's great love we are not [eaten up], for his compassions never fail. They are new every morning; great is your faithfulness."[33]

5. "Why should any living man complain when punished for his sins?[34] We should look at our behavior and go back to worshiping and obeying God. When I felt like I was in the bottom of a deep hole with no way out, I called out to God and he came near to me, telling me not to be afraid."

---

30. Lamentations 1:18.
31. Lamentations 2:11.
32. Lamentations 2:13-14.
33. Lamentations 3:22-23.
34. Lamentations 3:39.

6. "Lord, remember the awful things that have happened to us. You are king forever."

LEARNING FROM LAMENTATIONS

1. God's punishment is a terrible thing. It should remind us how bad *sin* is, and how important it is to love and obey God (See overview paragraphs 1–4).

   Bible references: Lamentations 1:18, 22; 1 Samuel 2:10; Romans 5:12.

   Questions: When your parents punish you, why do they do it? What are they hoping will be different after the punishment? Ask them about it!

2. It is right that sins are punished. It would not be fair if God ignored all the *sin* in the world. Even though Jeremiah was upset at all the suffering of the people, he knew that it was their own fault for disobeying and rejecting God, who had always protected and loved them (See overview paragraphs 1–2 and 5).

   Bible references: Lamentations 3:39; Psalm 94:2; Romans 3:23.
   Question: When someone robs a bank or kills someone do you think they should be punished? Why? When people disobey God by rejecting him, do you think it is fair if God punishes them? Why?

3. God is full of mercy and love. We should put our trust in him for the forgiveness of our sins (See overview paragraph 5).

   Bible references: Lamentations 3:22-23; Psalm 51:1; Ephesians 2:4-5.
   Question: Have you asked God to show you his love and his *mercy*, and forgive you for your sins?

SALVATION THREAD

Sin is massive and it brings death. God's *mercy* and love are even bigger, and they bring life. That's the message of the *gospel* and it's part of what Lamentations is about. Jeremiah understood that the *Israelites* deserved their terrible punishment from God (3:39), even though he didn't like the punishment and desperately wanted it to stop. He also knew that God doesn't enjoy punishing people (3:33), but had to punish the *Israelites* to help them see they needed to *repent* (3:40).

Jeremiah also knew that it was only God who could bring the *Israelites* out of the terrible problems caused by their *sin*. We need to remember that it is only God who can bring us out of the terrible problems caused by our *sin*.

Key Verse: "Because of the Lord's great love we are not consumed, for his compassions never fail. They are new every morning; great is your faithfulness" (Lamentations 3:22-23).

The book of
EZEKIEL

EZEKIEL

God's people heard, but they didn't listen

INTRODUCTION

- What would you say to people who are sad because people had forced them to leave their homes and everything they owned, and live in a far-off place where nobody liked them? What would you do if you had an important message but people wouldn't listen? This was Ezekiel's situation. God gave him visions with messages for God's people. Visions are like dreams, except you are awake and know it's a vision, not what is going on right now. Ezekiel was in Babylon at the time of his visions, when he was taken into exile after the first attack on Jerusalem.

- Ezekiel was a prophet from about 593 to 571 B.C.

OVERVIEW

1. "While I was in *exile* in Babylon, God gave me visions of himself. God told me to pass on some messages to the Israelites, and warned me that they would not believe me when I told them."

2. "God's first message was, 'I will punish you very severely like you deserve, for worshiping other gods, for disobeying me in other ways and not being sorry.'"

3. "'I will destroy those who make false prophecies, who say that I've told them the future when I haven't. And if someone has an idol in their heart I am not going to listen to what they want to ask me.'"

4. "'Instead, Ezekiel, make sure you tell them to repent and turn away from their idols. You need to be honest with them about their sin. Remind them that I have been patient and given them lots of chances to repent. Other countries will also be punished for their sins.'"

5. "God also said, 'When I punish people for being wicked, and when I gather the people of Israel back home, *they will know that I am the LORD.*'"[35]

6. "'My people come to you, Ezekiel, to listen to you; but all they want is to get more things and for you to say nice things to them. I will punish you,' God said to them, 'but one day *I will give you a new heart and ... move you to follow my decrees.*'"[36]

7. "God then took me in a vision to Jerusalem, showing me a new *temple*. He said that after the *exile*, people from other countries who made their home with God's people must be able to have land that they can pass on to their children."

8. "Last, God showed how the new city of Jerusalem should be built, and said that the name for the city would be, 'THE LORD IS THERE'" (Ezekiel 48:35).

---

35. Ezekiel 35:15.
36. Ezekiel 36:26-27.

LEARNING FROM EZEKIEL

1. God hates *sin*, and will punish it in the end. He is also full of love, and wants to save people from their sins. That is why he told the *Israelites* to *repent*, and it is why he tells us to *repent* (See overview paragraphs 2–4).

   Bible references: Ezekiel 33:11; Jeremiah 44:7-8; Revelation 2:21.

   Questions: What did the Israelites do wrong? Did God punish them straight away, or did he wait, giving lots of chances to repent? Why did he do that?

2. Sometimes people like to listen to teaching or preaching about the Bible, but only because they want someone to tell them everything is okay. But everything is not okay. That's why we need God. And that's why we should be kind to people and tell them what they need to hear, not just what they want to hear. Repenting means changing, but we must all do that (See overview paragraphs 3–4 and 6).

   Bible references: Ezekiel 33:31-32; James 1:22; 2 Timothy 4:3.

   Question: If someone was about to fall into a hole, would you say nothing because you didn't want them to get annoyed with you for telling them what to do? Or would you tell them to watch out so they didn't get hurt?

3. God wants people to know and understand that he is God. He shows his great love by rescuing them from their sins, and also by punishing sin. Here we see two parts of God: the holiness that hates sin, and the love that forgives it (See overview paragraphs 5–6).

   Bible references: Ezekiel 20:42, 23:49; 1 Kings 20:13; John 20:31.

   Question: Is it fair when people are punished for doing wrong? Is it great when people are rescued from danger? Imagine the wisest judge deciding a punishment and the best rescuer saving people from danger. God is like the wisest judge, and the best rescuer, all in one person.

SALVATION THREAD

The *Israelites* were God's chosen people, but they were not the only ones who God would forgive for their sins. This became clearer when Jesus came and said that, and even more clear when Paul the *apostle* became a missionary first to the Jews, but then to the Gentiles.

Even in the Old Testament we can see that God always meant to save people from all over the world. One example is when God told the *Israelites* to give land to foreigners who came to live with them (Ezekiel 47:22-23). By choosing to live with the *Israelites*, those foreigners were also choosing to worship God and join his people.

When the *Israelites* went home after *exile*, God promised that he would be with them. Every *Christian* all over the world – Jews and Gentiles – has God with them now. And one day God will be with us in *heaven*, which is the new Jerusalem.

Key Verse: "Say to them, 'As surely as I live, declares the Sovereign LORD, I take no pleasure in the death of the wicked, but rather that they turn from their ways and live. Turn! Turn from your evil ways! Why will you die, O house of Israel?'" (Ezekiel 33:11).

The book of
DANIEL

DANIEL

"God is my judge"[37]

INTRODUCTION

- Captured, plotted against, thrown in a den of lions and then in charge of a country. Daniel's life had some major highs and lows. God gave Daniel prophecies and told him the meanings of dreams. Daniel lived through the whole *exile*, from the time the *Israelites* were attacked by the Babylonians to when they started to return.

- Daniel was a prophet from about 605 to 536 B.C.

OVERVIEW

1. "King Nebuchadnezzar defeated the people of Judah at Jerusalem, and took the most talented men back to his country of Babylon, including Daniel and three of his friends: Hananiah, Mishael and Azariah."[38]

2. "Nebuchadnezzar had some dreams. No-one could explain them until Daniel was given the meanings by God. One dream meant that after four mighty empires, God would set in place a kingdom. It would start small, but grow to cover the earth and last forever. The king was amazed. He made Daniel an important ruler and said that Daniel's God was head of all gods."

3. "However, soon the king built a huge statue and told everyone to bow down and worship it. Daniel's three friends said no, so were thrown into a fire to be killed. However, God protected them. They walked around in the fire and it didn't hurt them. God later punished Nebuchadnezzar for his sins, and as a result the king praised and worshiped God."

4. "The Medes later conquered Babylon, but Daniel was still a ruler. Some jealous people tricked King Darius to make a law against praying to God, so when Daniel broke the law he was thrown into a pit of hungry lions. But God protected him and the lions left Daniel alone."

5. "God gave Daniel some special dreams and visions about what God would do with kings and countries. One dream had four beasts coming from the sea, but also *one like a son of man, coming with the clouds of heaven … He was given authority, glory and sovereign power …*"[39]

---

37. The name Daniel means, 'God is my judge'.
38. They were given new names by the Babylonians: Belteshazzar, Shadrach, Meshach and Abednego. All those names except Belteshazzar have meanings that worship the false gods of the Babylonians.
39. Daniel 7:13.

6. "Another dream was about a huge war: God's people will be attacked by a wicked king who thinks he is a god, but he will be defeated. At that time, the dead will be raised – *some to everlasting life, others to shame and everlasting contempt.*"[40]

LEARNING FROM DANIEL

1. God is in charge of all things. Even when it looks bad we can trust he still has his perfect plan (See overview paragraphs 2–5).

   Bible references: Daniel 2:20-21; 4:35; 5:26-28, 30; Jeremiah 25:9, 12; 1 Timothy 6:15.
   Questions: What happened in Daniel that shows God is in control? When bad things happen, is it possible God has lost control?

2. God's kingdom will last forever – everything else will end. Even the mighty Babylon was destroyed, so it is only God who can look after us (See overview paragraphs 2 and 5).

   Bible references: Daniel 2:44; Isaiah 51:9; Matthew 24:35; 2 Peter 3:10-13.
   Question: Who are the most important, best or strongest people or countries you can think of? If they all ended, who or what should we trust instead?

3. God's people will be with him forever in his kingdom, although there will be suffering and difficulties before we get there. Try to be like Daniel, who served God and didn't worry about what people thought about him (See overview paragraph 6).

   Bible references: Daniel 7:27; 12:1-3; 1 Peter 4:13; Revelation 21:3-4.
   Question: If God knows about the bad things that happen to us, and he has told us that they will happen, how much should we worry about them?

SALVATION THREAD

"In my vision at night I looked, and there before me was one like a son of man, coming with the clouds of *heaven*. He approached the Ancient of Days and was led into his presence. He was given authority, *glory* and sovereign power; all peoples, nations and men of every language worshiped him. His dominion is an everlasting dominion that will not pass away, and his kingdom is one that will never be destroyed" (Daniel 7:13-14).

Only Jesus fits this description of the 'son of man'. Only Jesus has been in the presence of God the Father and come to earth. Only he has authority and power over all creation. Only he has been appointed by the Father to be worshiped, and Jesus' kingdom is the only eternal kingdom. There are eighty-one examples in the gospels of Jesus calling himself the "Son of Man", which is a reference from Daniel.

Daniel lived when the world was dominated by warring empires. Each, for a time, looked unbeatable. This *prophecy* helps us understand that however powerful people, countries or empires may look, God is in charge. He sent his Son, Jesus Christ, as Savior of the world and Lord of all creation.

Key Verse: "… he is the living God and he endures for ever; his kingdom will never be destroyed, and his rule will never end. He rescues and he saves …" (Daniel 6:26-27, NLT).

---

40. Daniel 12:2.

MINOR PROPHETS

The book of
HOSEA

HOSEA

Unfaithful country, faithful God

INTRODUCTION

- Hosea was the last *prophet* in Israel before the Assyrian army destroyed the country in 722 B.C. He warned the people what would happen because of their constant *sin*. He was still alive when the punishment came. God made a picture of his people's sin through the life of Hosea. Hosea married a woman who breaks her promises to him just as Israel broke her promises to God. The woman is loved by Hosea to show that God loves his people.

- Hosea was a prophet for some time between 753 and 687 B.C.

OVERVIEW

1. "God said to Hosea, 'Go and marry a woman who will be unfaithful to you, because my people have been unfaithful to me.' So Hosea married Gomer, and they had children. God gave them names that would remind Hosea of God's plan to punish his people for their sins, although God would also save his people and bless them greatly."

2. "God said to me, '*Go show your love to your wife again,*[41] even though she has broken her promises to you by going with another man. *Love her as the* LORD *loves the Israelites, even though they turn to other gods and love [their sin].*'"[42]

3. "God said to the Israelites, 'There is no faithfulness here, no love, and no-one admits that I am God. There is awful sin everywhere; Israel is covered with it and you deny it. My people talk to an idol made from wood.'"

4. "'You must pay attention, Israel and Judah, because this judgment and punishment is against you and it will be awful when I turn away from you. You have boasted and relied on your own strength instead of on me, so you will be completely defeated. I loved Israel and brought them out of Egypt, but they went away from me to worship false gods and *they did not realize it was I who healed them.*[43] When I fed them they were satisfied, and when they were satisfied they became proud and forgot me.'"

5. "'*Return, Israel, to the* LORD *your God. Your sins have been your downfall!*[44] Say to God, '*Forgive all our sins and receive us graciously;*[45] other people can't save us. We will never again make things and call them gods.' Then, God says, '*I will … love [my people] freely, for my anger has turned away from them.*'"[46]

---

41. Hosea 3:1.
42. Hosea 3:1.
43. Hosea 11:3.
44. Hosea 14:1.
45. Hosea 14:2.
46. Hosea 14:4.

LEARNING FROM HOSEA

1. Telling Hosea to marry an unfaithful wife sounds unfair, until we realize that it is like what God has done for his people. They are faithless, and yet he chose them anyway and he remains faithful to them. That was true for the *Israelites* in 750 B.c, and it's true for Christians now (See overview paragraphs 1–2).

   Bible references: Hosea 3:1; 6:7; Deuteronomy 7:9; 2 Timothy 2:13.

   Questions: What can be more important to you than God? Would you like to repent of that to God now? If you are a Christian, think about how amazing it is that God chose you even though he knew you would not always keep your promises to him?

2. When people don't believe in God, they don't believe in nothing. Instead, they either believe in something that doesn't exist, or they believe in things or people that do exist but can't help them. The Israelites were praying to lumps of wood they called gods, and today many people believe they can fix their relationship with God just through good efforts (See overview paragraphs 2–3 and 5).

   Bible references: Hosea 4:12; 10:6b; Exodus 32:4; Psalm 40:4; Hebrews 13:6.

   Questions: What use were the false gods that the Israelites worshiped? What or who are you trusting in to make you right with God? Why?

3. God punished the Israelites severely because they worshiped false gods, disobeyed him, and did not repent of those sins. This reminds us that we must repent of our sins (See overview paragraph 5).

   Bible references: Hosea 4:1-3, 8; Proverbs 11:21; Revelation 3:3.

   Questions: Look at Hosea 13:1-9. What are some of the sins that the Israelites committed? Do any of those sins look like temptations for you?

SALVATION THREAD

"… I desire *mercy*, not *sacrifice*, and acknowledgement of God rather than burnt offerings" (Hosea 6:6).

Sometimes it might seem that a relationship with God in the Old Testament is all about doing the right things, and that forgiveness is gained by sacrificing animals. Actually it was never about that, and Jesus said that when he quoted this verse in Matthew 9:13. God wants people to *repent* (Hosea 14:1-2) and worship him as God. He wants us to love and be faithful to him, keeping him as the most important part of life. The sacrifices reminded God's people of their sin and their need for forgiveness, but did not remove the sins themselves (Hebrews 10:3-4) – only God can remove sin. (See also Psalm 40:6, Micah 6:6-8, Romans 3:23-26 and Hebrews 11:1-2).

Key Verse: "… it is time to seek the LORD, until he comes and showers righteousness on you" (Hosea 10:12).

The book of
JOEL

JOEL

God is bringing massive judgment and great blessing

INTRODUCTION

- Joel is a mystery man. We don't know who he was except that he was probably just an ordinary guy. He may have lived before, or possibly after God's people were taken into exile. God gave him a special message at a time of disaster, telling the people that they needed to repent because the terrible and wonderful "day of the LORD" was coming. The destruction caused by the locusts was awful, but it was just a little picture of what things will be like on "the day of the LORD".

- Joel was a prophet probably some time shortly after 586 B.C.

OVERVIEW

1. "The word of the LORD that came to Joel: 'Listen everyone. Has anything like this happened before? Tell your children about it, and Israel – remember what a terrible destruction was caused by the locusts. Everything is ruined and the people are terribly sad.'"

2. "'You need to *repent*! Cry out to God because *the day of the LORD*[47] is near, when destruction will come. God's army will come on that day and the universe will shake with fear about what that army can do ... *they leap over mountaintops ...*[48] and '*plunge through defenses.*'[49] Even now,' says God, '*repent*. Don't just do religious things. And bring everyone together to pray to God for his people, then God will take pity on them and destroy their enemies.'"

3. "God says about his people: 'Then you will praise the name of God, who has done amazing things for you, and you will know that I am in Israel, that I am the LORD your God, and that there is no other god. Then I will give the Holy Spirit to people everywhere, and *everyone who calls on the name of the LORD will be saved.*'"[50]

4. "'When I bring my people back to me, I will judge the nations,' God said. 'I will punish those who have gone against my people. The evil you have done to others will be done to you.'"

5. "'The day of the LORD is near. He will bring great fear to those who oppose him, but will be a place of protection for his people. Then you will know that I, the LORD your God, live with my people.'"

---

47. Joel 1:15.
48. Joel 2:5.
49. Joel 2:8.
50. Joel 2:32.

LEARNING FROM JOEL

1. God's message stays the same. He is coming and when he does he will bring his people to himself and put his enemies away forever. His people are those who have repented of their sins and received God's free gift of forgiveness. God loves to give this to everyone who really means it when they ask, and who aren't just trying to impress God by doing religious things (See overview paragraphs 3 and 6).

   Bible references: Joel 2:11-12; Jeremiah 18:8; Matthew 3:1-2; 4:17.

   Questions: What religious things do people do? Will those people be saved just because they do them? Are you asking God to forgive your sins, or are you trying to impress him?

2. The day of the LORD will be massive and amazing and scary and wonderful. If we have repented of our sins we can look forward to that day, but if we go against God it will be terrible (See overview paragraphs 3–6).

   Bible references: Joel 2:31-32; Malachi 4:1-2; Acts 2:2-21.

   Question: What is amazing about God's army? What does God do for his people?

3. The greatest thing that God does for his people is to give them himself. The most important difference between people is not their name, what they look like or where they're from. It's between those who are with God and those who are not. Being with God or without him is also the difference between heaven and hell (See overview paragraphs 4–6).

   Bible references: Joel 3:17; Deuteronomy 31:8; John 14:23.

   Questions: What kinds of things were happening to God's people when he was not with them? What would it be like when God was with them again? What does the book of Joel teach us about having God with you?

SALVATION THREAD

The day of Pentecost took place soon after Jesus went back to heaven. God gave the Holy Spirit to the *disciples*, who then started speaking in different languages. Some people who didn't know those languages wondered what was going on! In Acts chapter 2:16-21, the *apostle* Peter gave his great speech. He quoted the words of Joel from chapter 2:28-32 where he spoke about the Holy Spirit being given to all kinds of people.

Peter said that *prophecy* from Joel was coming true right there and then! Great miracles would happen, amazing things would take place, and everyone who called on God's name would be saved.

During the time of the Old Testament, God's Word mainly went out to the people of Israel. Only after Jesus came to earth did it go all over the world. Joel shows that, 500 years before Jesus, it was always God's plan for the gospel to go all over the world.

Key Verse: "Return to the LORD your God, for he is gracious and compassionate, slow to anger and abounding in love ..." (Joel 2:13).

The book of
AMOS

AMOS

God's people were too full of pride to see their own sin

INTRODUCTION

- Who would you pick to deliver terrible news? Maybe you would pick an important person who everyone knew? Or, someone who was used to giving bad news? On this occasion, God chose a poor person with no relevant experience: a shepherd, who also looked after fig trees. It was a scary thing to do but Amos obeyed God and gave the message of bad news to the people. What made it an even more difficult message was that life seemed to be going really well in Israel. Because it was going well, most people thought God was giving them a reward for obeying him, and that he would come soon to help them wipe out all their enemies.

- Amos was a prophet for some time between 793 and 739 B.C.

OVERVIEW

1. "The words of Amos: The LORD roars and thunders."

2. "This is what God says: 'I will send fire and destruction on those who have acted in an evil way, like the nations of Ekron and Moab who attacked others out of greed for things and for land.'"

3. "'My people of Judah will also be severely punished, because they rejected my law and worship false gods. They hate the truth, treat poor people badly and are unfair to those who need help and protection. I rescued them from Egypt and defeated their enemies, but they rejected my many warnings about their behavior.'"

4. "God says to them, 'I chose you out of all the countries in the world, so *I will punish you for all your sin.*[51] I hate all the religious things you are doing, the offerings and the songs. You are worshiping false gods and therefore I will send you into *exile* and only a tiny part of your country will survive. So, seek me and live.'"

5. "'You think everything is going to be okay because life feels good now. You think I like what you're doing, but it's horrible. You think you are so great, but you are not.'"

6. "When Amos passed on these messages, a priest called Amaziah told King Jereboam that Amos was making a bad plan against him by saying these things. So, the King sent Amos out of Israel, into Judah."

7. "God said, 'It is time for me to punish my people. Because of all their evil I will take my words away from them. I will destroy that sinful country of Israel, but I will not

---
51. Amos 3:2.

totally destroy them. Then later, at the same time as evil is being punished, I will bring my people back to me.'"

LEARNING FROM AMOS

1. The Israelites needed to learn that just because life seemed to be going well, it didn't mean that they were right with God. We need to pay attention to how we are living and whether we are really worshiping God, instead of just saying that we do, or just going to church (See overview paragraphs 3–5).

    Bible references: Amos 5:18; 6:1; Zephaniah 1:12-13; Matthew 3:7-10.

    Questions: Do you ask God to help you see the *sin* in your life? Are you sometimes tempted to think everything's okay as long as you don't get caught doing something wrong?

2. People don't like to be told that they are doing bad things, or that they need to change. Even people who say they love God can be like this, like the *priest* Amaziah who got Joel in trouble with the king. We should ask God for help, so that when we are shown our *sin* we are sorry to God (See overview paragraphs 3 and 6).

    Bible references: Amos 7:10-13; 1 Samuel 12:13; Jeremiah 20:1-2; Mark 6:17-20.

    Question: What do you do when your parents or teacher tells you that you have done something wrong? Are you sad because of your sin or do you get angry at the person who told you? Ask God for help with that.

3. God's Word is precious and without it we cannot know God. To have God's Word taken away would be a terrible thing (See overview paragraph 7).

    Bible references: Amos 8:11-13; Psalm 19:9-11; Matthew 4:4; Acts 7:41-42.

    Question: What do you think your body would feel like if you were not able to eat or drink anything for two days? Without God's Word, that's what it is like for your soul.

SALVATION THREAD

Jesus' brother James was in a meeting with Peter and other important people in Jerusalem, after Jesus had gone back to heaven. They were trying to decide whether all the non-Jews (Gentiles) should obey all the Jewish laws that God gave to Moses many years before.

Peter said no, they shouldn't have to. God was already saving them from their sins, and gave them the Holy Spirit, without them obeying the parts of the *law* about special days and sacrifices and so on.

James agreed with Peter, and used a quote from Amos 9:11-13 as evidence. In Acts 15:16-17 Peter said it like this: "The rest of mankind may seek the Lord, even all the Gentiles who are called by my name, says the Lord …" When Amos wrote that, about 800 years before Peter, God still spoke mainly to his chosen people - the Jews. But a time was coming when God's good news would go all over the world. That time came after Jesus' death and resurrection.

Key Verse: "Hear this word the LORD has spoken against you, O people of Israel – against the whole family I brought up out of Egypt" (Amos 3:1).

The book of
OBADIAH

OBADIAH

A warning to God's enemies

INTRODUCTION

- Obadiah's name was a common one for Old Testament times and it doesn't seem that he was very important. He probably wrote this *prophecy* after Babylon defeated Judah and took them into captivity. His *prophecy* was for God's people, and it was about the nation of Edom, descended from Jacob's brother Esau. The book is the shortest in the Old Testament.

- Obadiah was a prophet for some time between 586 and 553 B.C.

OVERVIEW

1. "This is what the Sovereign LORD says about Edom: 'A message has come from the LORD to all the countries to say, "*Come, let us go and do battle against Edom.*" I will make you small and people will think you are nothing. You have been tricked by your own pride and it will be your downfall. You think no-one can do anything bad to you but terrible things will happen to you. You will lose everything. Your friends will betray and defeat you and you won't see it coming. Your wise men will be destroyed, your soldiers that you think will keep you safe will be scared, and your people will be killed.'"

2. "Because of your violence against God's people – your brothers – everyone will look down on you and you will be destroyed forever. When you watched people destroy Jerusalem and did nothing to help, it was as bad as doing it yourself. You should not have been pleased that Judah, God's people, suffered. You should not have stolen from them, or killed them while they were trying to flee their attackers, or handed them over to their enemies."

3. "God will come again and judge all the countries. What you have done to other people will be done to you. Everyone who has gone against God will be punished by him forever."

4. "But God will save his people, he will make them *holy* and they will receive their reward."

5. "God will own and rule over everything."

LEARNING FROM OBADIAH

1. God hates *pride*, and all *sin*. *Pride* is thinking that you are better or more important than you are (See overview paragraph 1).

   Bible references: Obadiah 3, 4, 8, 9; Proverbs 11:2; Romans 12:3.

   Questions: What are you tempted to feel proud about? Are you proud about what you are good at? Or where you are from? Or what you have?

2. God saved Israel from many enemies. God will rescue his people. God even saves his people from themselves – to turn away from God is to hurt yourself and God can stop that. That's why verse 17 talks about God making his people *holy* and giving them their reward (*heaven*). Ask God to help you to be *holy* and not to turn away from him (See overview paragraph 4).

   Bible references: Obadiah 17; Galatians 1:4,13; 2 Peter 2:9.

   Questions: What bad things happened to God's people that Obadiah was talking about? Might this have made the *Israelites* think God didn't care any more? Or that he couldn't help? Do you ever think God doesn't care about you?

3. God is the King now and he will be King forever. He is in charge of everything.

   Bible references: Obadiah 21; Isaiah 33:22; Jude 24-25.

   Questions: What bad things do you see people do, and seem to get away with? What does Obadiah say will happen to all the "countries" (that means everyone) in the end?

SALVATION THREAD

Obadiah's theme was that there will be judgment on those who reject God, but *salvation* for God's people. Because of Edom's *pride*, that country will be made "small among the nations; you will be utterly despised,"[52] but "the house of Jacob will possess its inheritance"[53]

The last verse of the prophecy is the climax to all that God is doing: "the kingdom will be the LORD's."[54] If we love God and he is our Savior, this is a great comfort and encouragement. If we reject God, then it serves as a warning.

Most importantly, like all prophecy in the Bible, it was true.

Key Verse: "Deliverers will go up on Mount Zion to govern the mountains of Esau. And the kingdom will be the LORD's" (Obadiah 21).

---

52. Obadiah 2.
53. Obadiah 17.
54. Obadiah 21.

The book of
JONAH

JONAH

God hates sin, but loves sinners

INTRODUCTION

- The city of Nineveh, in Assyria, was full of sin. Its people worshiped false gods, attacked and killed thousands of people, and boasted about it. That included cruelty to God's people, the Israelites. If you had to pick the most evil people in the world in 800 B.C., you might have picked them. It was to those people that God sent a warning through the prophet Jonah, giving them an opportunity to repent and turn to him. However, Jonah didn't want to go to Nineveh …

- Jonah was a prophet possibly for some time between 782 and 753 B.C.

OVERVIEW

1. "God said to Jonah, 'Go to the great city of Nineveh and preach against it,'[55] because of their terrible sin. But Jonah ran away from God and got on a boat heading in the opposite direction. God sent a storm so big that it looked like the boat would break. All the sailors were scared and started praying to their false gods. But Jonah said it was his fault for disobeying God. He made them throw him off the boat. Then the storm became calm, and the sailors – who were still on the boat – made sacrifices to God. Meanwhile, God sent a big fish to swallow Jonah."

2. "From inside the fish, Jonah prayed: 'I was in great danger and about to die, but you saved me. You threw me deep into the sea, but I prayed to you and you answered me. Only you can save, and I will serve you.' Then God made the fish spit Jonah out onto a beach.

3. "Again, God gave Jonah a message for the Ninevites. This time, Jonah obeyed and the people of Nineveh repented, turning away from their *sin*. God had compassion on them and did not destroy them. This made Jonah angry because he wanted them punished for the evil they had done. Jonah told God that was why he had run away. '*I knew that you are a gracious and compassionate God, slow to anger and abounding in love.*'[56] He said he knew that God was going to forgive them and that he'd rather die than put up with that!"

4. "Jonah went out of the city and made himself a shelter from the sun so that he could watch what happened to Nineveh. God provided a plant that grew in one night and gave him shade, but next day God made the plant die. Jonah got angry again, and said to God that he'd rather be dead."

---

55. Jonah 1:1.
56. Jonah 4:2.

5. "God said, '*You have been concerned about this [plant], though you did not tend it or make it grow. It sprang up overnight and died overnight. But Nineveh has more than a hundred and twenty thousand people*[57] who don't know me – should I not be concerned about them?'"

LEARNING FROM JONAH

1. God is full of compassion and patience and is willing to forgive anyone who repents; God forgave the Ninevites, who did terrible things. Nothing that you have done is so bad that God can't or won't forgive you (See overview paragraphs 3 and 5).

    Bible references: Jonah 3:10; 4:11; Jeremiah 33:8; Luke 5:31-32.
    Questions: Which two groups of people in the story of Jonah turned away from their sin to God? Can you think of other people in the Bible who did very bad things but were forgiven by God? Do you believe that God will forgive you if you ask him?

2. God is in control of all things. In this story we can see that he directed the weather, the actions of a huge fish, and the people of Nineveh. That means when God makes promises, we have an excellent reason to trust him (See overview paragraphs 1–2 and 4).

    Bible references: Jonah 1:2-10, 15-16; Exodus 14:31; John 20:31.
    Questions: What did God do to the weather, the big fish and the people of Nineveh? How did the sailors know that Jonah's God was real? (See Jonah 1:15). How can you know that God is real?

3. People who look like they are religious, or do good things, need forgiveness just as much as everyone else. Jonah was a *prophet* of God but we can see his *sin* (See overview paragraphs 1–5).

    Bible references: Jonah 4:1-4, 9, 11; Micah 3:1-2a; Luke 10:30-33.
    Question: What did Jonah do that was wrong? How did he feel about evil people? Did he want God to save them from their sins or just to punish them? How do you feel about people you think are nasty?

SALVATION THREAD

Jesus said that Jonah was a sign to the Ninevites in the same way that Jesus was a sign to the people in his own time. Jonah spent three days in the stomach of a big fish. Everyone thought he was dead. It was like he came to life again when the fish spat him back onto dry land. Jesus died, his friends thought he was gone forever, but three days later God raised him from the dead (Matthew 12:39-41; Luke 18:31-33).

Key Verse: "Those who cling to worthless idols turn away from God's love for them … *Salvation* comes from the LORD" (Jonah 2:8–9).

---

57. Jonah 4:10-11.

The book of
MICAH

MICAH

God judges and forgives

INTRODUCTION

- You would need great courage to go to a Prime Minister or President and say their country was going to be destroyed because of their evil behavior. That's what God told Micah to do, and the prophet needed 'power' from the Holy Spirit"[58] to do it. Micah lived at the same time as the prophets Isaiah and Hosea, in the southern kingdom of Judah. He warned about what was soon going to happen in Israel – the northern kingdom.

- Micah was a prophet for about 20-25 years during the period 750 to 687 B.C.

OVERVIEW

1. "Listen everyone: God is speaking against you. 'I will make the city of Samaria a pile of rubble and all her idols will be smashed. Cry for your children, because they will be taken into *exile*. Woe to those who plan evil like stealing and cheating. You have ruined the land with your sin, so I will bring a disaster that you can't save yourself from. You will be taken away from your country, but one day I will bring people back.'"

2. "Then I, Micah, said to the leaders: 'You should know justice, but you hate goodness and love evil. You sit back and say God is with us, everything will be OK, but it is because of you that the country will be destroyed. When you are punished for your terrible sins against the people, you will cry to God for help but he will turn away from you. The false prophets say whatever people pay them to say, and they tell God's prophets to be quiet. God says he won't talk to the prophets any more, and won't answer their questions.'"

3. "In the last days many people will want to go to the mountain of God's temple so that God can teach them to follow him. God's Word will go out from Jerusalem to the nations and it will bring peace between different people, who will not be afraid any more."

4. "*You will go to Babylon; there you will be rescued. There the* LORD *will redeem you out of the hand of your enemies.*[59] But right now, other countries are lining up against you – they don't know what I have planned because in the end you will destroy them."

5. "Israel will be abandoned until all God's people return and the great ruler shepherds his flock in God's strength and majesty. God will give his people peace and safety."

---

58. Micah 3:8.
59. Micah 4:10.

6. "'I will destroy your idols,' God says, 'so that you no longer worship things you have made, and I will punish the nations that have not obeyed me.'"

LEARNING FROM MICAH

1. God is *holy* and will not put up with *sin* forever (See overview paragraphs 1 and 2).

   Bible references: Micah 2:1-3; Nehemiah 9:29-30; Romans 2:5.

   Question: What are the different punishments that God talked about in Micah?

2. God is a forgiving God who loves his people. Even when he was in the middle of telling Israel about the punishment for their *sin*, he also spoke about how he would bless them and bring them back when their punishment was over (See paragraphs 1, 3–6).

   Bible references: Micah 5:3-5; Psalm 99:8-9; Galatians 3:22.

   Question: What are the blessings that God promises his people in Micah?

3. People keep sinning for different reasons. Sometimes it is because they think God doesn't know what we think. Or they imagine he doesn't care, or is only interested in making sure we do things like go to church and give money. Or they simply love to *sin* (See overview paragraphs 1–2).

   Bible references: Micah 3:1-2; 6:7-8; Jeremiah 16:10-12; Romans 8:5.

   Questions: How do you feel about your *sin*? How do you think God feels about it?

SALVATION THREAD

When King Herod, in a panic about the news of the wise men, asked the Jewish teachers where the Messiah/Savior would be born, this verse told them the answer (quoted in Matthew 2:1-6):

"But you, Bethlehem Ephrathah, though you are small among the clans of Judah, out of you will come for me one who will be ruler over Israel, whose origins are from of old, from ancient times" (Micah 5:2).

That is why God went to the trouble to make sure that Mary was in Bethlehem (Joseph's home town) when she gave birth to Jesus (Luke 2:1-5).

But Micah didn't just tell us where the Messiah would be born, but also what he would do. He said that the ruler would be a shepherd for his people, in God's strength and for God's glory. The greatness of the ruler would spread over the whole world and he would keep his people safe.

That ruler is Jesus Christ, and you can be part of his people!

Key Verse: "Who is a pardoning God like you, who pardons sin ...? You do not stay angry for ever but delight to show mercy" (Micah 7:18).

The book of
NAHUM

NAHUM

God will not put up with sin forever

INTRODUCTION

- Nineveh was a wicked and well-defended city. God said he would destroy it, and sent his *prophet* Jonah to warn the people who lived there. They repented of their sin, and God did not destroy them. However, 100 years later the people of Nineveh went back to their idol-worshiping, violent, and murderous ways and God decided they must be stopped. People need to see that he does not put up with sin forever. So Nahum didn't call people to repentance, he just announced that a terrible destruction would happen. Fifty years after Nahum's prophecy, God's Word came true when Nineveh was wiped out by armies from Mede and Babylon. Nahum's prophecy comforted to God's people, the *Israelites*. They were attacked by the powerful Ninevites and could not imagine their enemy being defeated.

- Nahum was a prophet for some time between 664 and 612 B.C.

OVERVIEW

1. "The LORD severely punishes his enemies. He is slow to anger and great in power. He is so full of power and his punishments are so terrible, it is like the mountains are scared and the hills get out of his way."

2. "God is good and a place of safety, but he will destroy Nineveh because they plot against him and encourage people to *sin*. God says, 'I will free my people from the terrible things you do to them.' The LORD has given a command about you, Nineveh: 'I am going to end you and destroy your idols. Peace will come to Judah, where my people live – now, people of Judah: celebrate your festivals and keep your promises to me!'"

3. "An attacker is coming for you, Nineveh – get ready to defend yourself with everything you've got. God will make Israel a great country again, though they have suffered many attacks and much destruction. The palace of Nineveh will collapse and those who live in the city will be taken away. *Nineveh is like a pool, and its water is draining away.*[60] 'I am against you,' says God, 'I will burn up your chariots in smoke.'"[61]

4. "God says, 'Woe to Nineveh, which is full of violence, stealing, lies and killing. Are you better than the other mighty cities I have defeated? No. Your strong troops will be useless and will run away from your enemy, who will destroy you with fire and the sword.'"

5. "'Nothing can heal your injury – it will lead to your death. All those who hear the news about you being destroyed will be glad, because you have been cruel to everyone.'"

---

60. Nahum 2:8.
61. Nahum 2:13.

LEARNING FROM NAHUM

1. God does not ignore *sin* forever – in the end he will punish it. He gave the people of Nineveh many chances to *repent*, but after years of idol worship and killings, he punished them. Some people think that when God doesn't punish them straight away it's because he never will. But really, he is giving them more chances to repent before judgment comes (See overview paragraphs 1–4).

    Bible references: Nahum 1:3; 4:19; Exodus 34:6-7; 2 Peter 3:9-10.

    Questions: How did the Ninevites feel about their *sin*? How does God feel about *sin*? How do you feel about *sin*?

2. God's punishments are terrible and unstoppable, and we cannot imagine how bad they can be. That's what Nahum prophesied against Nineveh, and all those who go against God (See overview paragraphs 1–4).

    Bible references: Nahum 1:2 and 6; Jeremiah 10:10; Hebrews 10:31; Revelation 16:19-20.

    Questions: If the Ninevites heard and believed Nahum's prophecy, what would they have done? How would you react to a *prophecy* about punishment coming from God?

3. God will always look after his people, and bring them through bad times into a time of amazing blessing. Christians can enjoy God's blessings now, as well as look forward to the great blessing of heaven, when we will have peace forever (See overview paragraphs 2–4).

    Bible references: Nahum 1:7, 12; Jeremiah 31:23; Acts 3:26.

    Questions: How did God promise that he would bless Israel? How do you feel about God, who gives such great punishments and blessings?

SALVATION THREAD

"What if God, choosing to show his wrath and make his power known, bore with great patience the objects of his wrath – prepared for destruction? What if he did this to make the riches of his *glory* known to the objects of his *mercy*, whom he prepared in advance for *glory* – even us, whom he also called, not only from the Jews but also from the Gentiles?" (Romans 9:22-24).

Nahum reminds us that God is a *holy* God who does not leave *sin* unpunished. Also, he is a loving God who will one day bring his people into everlasting peace … even though they don't deserve it.

God punished his people so that they would realize their own sinfulness, and *repent*. God used the Ninevites for that, but the Ninevites just loved to kill and steal from people. They did not love God and did not treat people fairly. God put up with their *sin* for a long time before destroying them. This showed how merciful God had been to his people in not destroying them for their sin, which is what they deserved (Psalm 103:10).

Like the Ninevites and the *Israelites*, we deserve punishment and not *mercy*. But, the good news of forgiveness is that if we *repent* of our sins, then God will show us *mercy* – he will forgive us (Titus 3:3-7).

Key Verse: "The LORD is slow to anger and great in power; the LORD will not leave the guilty unpunished" (Nahum 1:3).

The book of
HABAKKUK

HABAKKUK

How long must I wait for justice?

INTRODUCTION

- Habakkuk was confused and upset. Wicked people got their own way and God would let them defeat his people, the *Israelites*. Why? Habakkuk wasn't shy about telling God how he felt. God replied that things would get worse before they got better, because the people were disobedient. God's message of bad times to come, made the prophet unpopular.

- Habakkuk was a prophet around the time 612 to 585 B.C.

OVERVIEW

1. "'*How long, O* Lord, *must I call for help but you do not listen? ...Why do you make me look at injustice? Why do you tolerate wrong?*'"[62] asked Habakkuk.

2. "'Watch,' said God. 'I am going to do something you wouldn't believe. I am raising up the Babylonians, a wicked people interested only in themselves, who are feared and great in battle. They are *guilty men, whose own strength is their god.*'"[63]

3. "Habakkuk replied, 'God, you have chosen the Babylonians to punish the wicked, but they are more wicked than the ones you are punishing! Why do you put up with them?'"

4. God said to him, 'Write down the revelation – it will come true at a time I have set and will not be delayed. The wicked are boastful and don't want what is right, *but the righteous will live by his faith.*'[64] The greedy are never satisfied. They take captives and steal from many people. One day those captives will rise up and attack their captors. Woe to those who get rich through evil behavior. They go against God, but for nothing in the end. *For the earth will be filled with the knowledge of the glory of the* Lord *as the waters cover the sea.*'"[65]

5. "*Of what value is an idol, since a man has carved it? ... Can it give guidance? ... there is no breath in it. But the* Lord *is in his holy temple; let all the earth be silent before him.*"[66]

6. "Habakkuk prayed: 'Lord, you have done awesome things in the past. Do them again now; remember mercy even though you are angry about sin. God's glory covered the skies ... He stood, and shook the earth; he looked, and made the nations tremble ... His ways are eternal.'"[67]

7. "You came out to deliver your people ... You crushed the leader of the land of wickedness ...[68] Even though we are without food, I will wait patiently for God to defeat our enemy ... *I will rejoice in the* Lord."[69]

---

62. Habakkuk 1:2-3.
63. Habakkuk 1:11.
64. Habakkuk 2:4.
65. Habakkuk 2:14.
66. Habakkuk 2:18-20.
67. Habakkuk 3:6.
68. Habakkuk 3:13.
69. Habakkuk 3:18.

LEARNING FROM HABAKKUK

1. Habakkuk thought God was waiting too long to bring justice and save his people. He needed to learn patience, and that God always does things at the right time (See overview paragraphs 1, 3, 6–7).

   Bible references: Habakkuk 1:2-5; Psalms 37:7; Revelation 6:10-11.

   Questions: Have you seen people being rude, cheating, or lying, but get away with it? Have you asked God to fix something, or punish people for doing wrong things, and he didn't do it straight away?

2. God always does what is best and right, even if we don't agree with it. Habakkuk couldn't understand why God would use the wicked Babylonians to punish God's own people, the Israelites (See overview paragraphs 2–4 and 7).

   Bible references: Habakkuk 1:5-6; Isaiah 55:8-9; Romans 8:28.

   Questions: What has happened to you, or in the world, that you don't think is fair? Who in the Bible had things happen to them that seem unfair?

3. God is sovereign, which means he is in control of all things. Since he always does the right and best thing at the perfect time, we should thank and praise him (See overview paragraphs 2–4 and 7).

   Bible references: Habakkuk 3:18-19; Daniel 4:37; Matthew 6:9-10.

   Question: How do you feel about God, who does the best thing at the best time and is always in control?

SALVATION THREAD

"My soul glorifies the Lord and my spirit rejoices in God my Savior, for he has been mindful of the humble state of his servant. From now on all generations will call me blessed, for the Mighty One has done great things for me – *holy* is his name. His *mercy* extends to those who fear him, from generation to generation. He has performed mighty deeds with his arm; he has scattered those who are proud in their inmost thoughts. He has brought down rulers from their thrones but has lifted up the humble" (Mary the mother of Jesus, in Luke 1:46-52).

"Lord I have heard of your fame; I stand in awe of your deeds, O Lord … in wrath remember *mercy* … You came to deliver your people … You crushed the leader of the land of wickedness … I will rejoice in the Lord, I will be joyful in God my Savior. The Sovereign Lord is my strength; he makes my feet like the feet of a deer, he enables me to go on the heights" (Habakkuk 3:2, 13, 18-19).

Mary's words were written about 620 years after Habakkuk's words from God, and they're saying the same things about the same God. That's because God is the same forever: showing mercy to his people, punishing sin and doing mighty things in the world. Now, 2,000 years after Mary, God is still the same. So if Habakkuk could praise God, and Mary could praise God, then we should praise God too.

Key Verse: "I will rejoice in the Lord, I will be joyful in God my Savior. The sovereign Lord is my strength …" (Habakkuk 3:18-19).

The book of
ZEPHANIAH

ZEPHANIAH

God has protected[70]

INTRODUCTION

- How many chances did the people of Judah want? How many warnings did they need? The Assyrians destroyed the northern kingdom (Israel) about 100 years earlier but Judah (the southern kingdom) still did not repent of their sins. Zephaniah was one of the last prophets sent by God before the Babylonian invasion. He spoke to the people during the reign of King Josiah, who tried to turn the people back to God.

- Zephaniah was a prophet for some time during 640-609 B.C.

OVERVIEW

1. "God said, '*I will sweep away everything from the face of the earth.*[71] The only thing left for wicked people will be piles of rubble. I will punish Judah. I will get rid of all the idols and those who worship them; those who fill the country with violence and lying. I will punish those who think I won't do anything.'"

2. "'The day of the LORD is coming soon. I will bring sadness and pain because the people have sinned against the LORD, and their money won't be able to save them. Countries will be abandoned and destroyed, but God will care for his people. You must seek God and obey him before it's too late.'"

3. "God says, 'I have heard the insults of Moab against my people and I will make Moab a wasteland forever … This is what they will get in return for their pride, for insulting and mocking the people of the LORD Almighty …[72] But people from all over the world will worship God.'"

4. "Assyria will be destroyed, including its capital Nineveh. They thought they were great but they will become a ruin. They obey no-one, they don't accept correction, and they don't trust the LORD. God is righteous and does no wrong; he does not fail. He said to Nineveh, 'Surely you will respect me and turn away from your *sin*! Then there will be no punishment from me. But they still wanted to carry on in their sins.'"

5. "'So I will punish the world,' said God. 'I will clean people from their *sin* so they can worship and serve me. I will take away those who are proud, but I will leave those who are humble and who trust in me. My people will be made perfect; they will rejoice because I have taken away their punishment and they don't need to be afraid of anything. God is with you; he will rescue the injured and sick, and bring all his people back home.'"

---

70. Zephaniah means 'God has protected'.
71. Zephaniah 1:2.
72. Zephaniah 2:8-10.

LEARNING FROM ZEPHANIAH

1. Nothing can save people from God's punishment except God. Many of the *Israelites* didn't believe this so they ignored God's warnings. Today, some people wrongly think that they will be okay because they have lots of money, or they have *Christian* parents, or believe they do the right things (See overview paragraphs 1–5).

   Bible references: Zephaniah 3:8; 2 Chronicles 19:7; Galatians 2:6.

   QUESTIONS: Do you get angry because you think some people have an unfair advantage? Thank God that no-one has an unfair advantage with him!

2. God will bless people from all over the world – not just the *Israelites*, or people from the same country as you. Not just people who speak your language, or people who look like you or who like the things you like. (See overview paragraphs 3–5).

   Bible references: Zephaniah 3:9-20; Psalm 72:17; Galatians 3:8.

   QUESTIONS: Who do you think most needs to hear the good news of forgiveness? Does anyone need it more than anyone else, or do we all need it just the same?

3. God will remove all the *sin* from the world. That means he will forgive the sins of many people so that they become God's people. He will punish those who love sin – people who will not be sorry and ask for forgiveness (See overview paragraphs 3–5).

   Bible references: Zephaniah 3:6-9; Ezekiel 20:38; 2 Thessalonians 1:8-10.

   QUESTION: What would it be like to live in a world without *sin*?

SALVATION THREAD

"The great day of the LORD is near … That day will be a day of wrath … a day of darkness and gloom, a day of clouds and blackness … I will bring distress on the people … because they have sinned against the LORD … In the fire of his jealousy the whole world will be consumed …" (Zephaniah 1:14–18).

"But the day of the Lord will come like a thief. The heavens will disappear with a roar; the elements will be destroyed by fire, and the earth and everything in it will be laid bare" (2 Peter 3:10).

Many prophecies in the Old Testament talk about the "day of the LORD". Zephaniah and other prophets talked about two things about that day: a terrible punishment that would happen, and the day of judgment when Jesus would come again. Peter, who wrote a letter after Jesus had gone to *heaven*, wrote about an attack by the *Romans* (this happened in A.D. 72) and the day of judgment when Jesus would come again.

The "day of the LORD" or the day of judgment will be a terrible and scary time when *sin* is punished. But it will also be a wonderful day for God's people when he will bring them home to be with him forever, taking away all punishment and all suffering.[73]

Key Verse: "The LORD your God is with you, he is mighty to save" (Zephaniah 3:17).

---

73. Zephaniah 3:13-20.

The book of
HAGGAI

HAGGAI

Learning to put God first

INTRODUCTION

- At last, the *Israelites* were allowed to return home, and rebuild God's *temple* and Jerusalem. However, some people discouraged and threatened the *Israelites*, who then stopped their work on the temple. Instead, they built nice houses for themselves and forgot about their work for God.

- Haggai received God's Word from August to December 520 B.C.

OVERVIEW

1. "God's message came through Haggai to Zerubbabel (governor of Israel) and Joshua (the *High priest*). God said, 'These people say it's not yet time to rebuild God's house (the *temple*). But is it time to be living in your fancy houses while God's house is still a ruin? Think about what you are doing. You are working hard to try and get things for yourselves but it's not going well. I am not letting you succeed with being greedy, because I want you to change. Go and get wood and rebuild the *temple* so that I will be honored.'"

2. "After this, the leaders and the people obeyed God and respected him greatly. They knew that God had sent Haggai and they started to rebuild the *temple*. Then Haggai gave this message from God: '*I am with you*.'"[74]

3. "'Be strong,' God said to them a month later, 'and keep going. *For I am with you*,[75] just as I promised when you came out of Egypt. Do not fear.'"[76]

4. "'*In a little while I will once more shake the heavens and the earth … the desired of all nations will come, and I will fill this house with glory …The glory of this present house will be greater than the glory of the former house … And in this place I will grant peace*,'[77] declares the LORD Almighty."

5. "'Remember, I punished you to remind you to *repent* but you did not turn back to me. You have nothing now, but you are starting to build my *temple*.'"

6. "'From this day on I will bless you.'[78] Then Haggai gave a message from God to Zerubbabel: 'I will come and shake the earth, and will take you and use you greatly, for I have chosen you.'"

---

74. Haggai 2:4.
75. Haggai 1:13.
76. Haggai 2:5.
77. Haggai 2:6-9.
78. Haggai 2:19.

LEARNING FROM HAGGAI

1. It's easy to think about what we want, or think we need, and forget that the most important thing is to serve God. When the *Israelites* were allowed to go back to Israel after *exile*, the main thing they wanted was to be comfortable again in their own houses. They were not that interested in loving and honoring God by rebuilding his house (the *temple*) first (See overview paragraphs 1–2).

   Bible references: Haggai 1:2-3, 7-9; Psalm 119:60; Luke 9:59-60.

   Questions: What is important to you? Do you think it is important to God?

2. God doesn't leave his people in their sin and ignore them; he helps them come back to him. The *Israelites* were more interested in their own things, so God made sure they didn't succeed. When they still didn't repent, he sent Haggai to tell them what was wrong, and to encourage them to love and obey God (See overview paragraphs 1, 2 and 5).

   Bible references: Haggai 2:14-17; Jeremiah 7:13; Hebrews 12:4-6.

   Question: Can you think of a time when you realized you were disobedient to God, and then became sorry about it? That was God's kindness to you – helping you to see what was wrong and encouraging you to love and obey Him.

3. God is with his people and loves to encourage them. One big way he does that is by promises to be with them. God didn't wait until after the Israelites finished the temple, before he promised to be with them. He made that promise (which he'd been making ever since they came out of Egypt), as soon as they started building. God is with his people now. He wants their repentance and love, and he knows they're not perfect yet! (See overview paragraphs 2–6).

   Bible references: Haggai 2:4-5; 1 Chronicles 28:20; Romans 8:31.

   Question: If God waited for you to be perfect before being with you, when do you think he would be with you?

SALVATION THREAD

God promised through Haggai that he would "shake"[79] the countries. This was a prophecy about the fall of empires. Also that when the temple was rebuilt it would be filled again with wonderful things, and God would be there. Then it says, "The *glory* of this present house will be greater than the *glory* of the former house," says the LORD Almighty. "And in this place I will grant peace," declares the LORD Almighty.[80]

God wasn't just talking about what would happen in Israel's history, he was also talking about Jesus' return. Hebrews 12:28 says, "we are receiving a kingdom that cannot be shaken", so God's people should "be thankful, and so worship God" with great respect. And that God's people are protected and saved by an awesome and powerful God.

Key Verse: "Be strong, all you people of the land … and work. For I am with you," declares the LORD Almighty. "This is what I covenanted with you when you came out of Egypt. And my Spirit remains among you. Do not fear" (Haggai 2:4-5).

---

79. Haggai 2:7.
80. Haggai 2:9.

The book of
ZECHARIAH

ZECHARIAH

When serving God seems pointless

INTRODUCTION

- Sometimes doing the right thing feels too difficult. The *Israelites* knew they were supposed to rebuild the *temple* and city. But they were forced to give lots of money to foreign rulers, and many people tried to stop their building work, so they gave up. But God reminded them about him and his plans, to encourage them. He sent his message through a priest called Zechariah, who lived at the same time as the *prophet* Haggai.

- Zechariah prophesied from 520 B.C. until possibly around 495 B.C.

OVERVIEW

1. "'Return to me and I will return to you,'[81] said God to the *Israelites*. Don't be like those before you who did not listen or pay attention to me – they were punished."

2. "Zechariah received visions from God. In one, Joshua the *High priest* was standing in front of the angel of the LORD, with *Satan* there to accuse Joshua of sin. God said, '*The LORD rebuke you, Satan!*'[82] He said to Joshua, '*See, I have taken away your sin.*'"[83]

3. "Another vision had four chariots pulled by powerful horses, coming out from between two mountains of bronze. The angel said, 'The chariots are the four spirits of *heaven*,' and God said 'Joshua will build God's *temple*, and there will be peace if you obey him.'"

4. "People asked God whether they should still *fast*. God asked them, 'Were you really doing it for me or just for your own good?' God also said, 'Treat people fairly, *show mercy and compassion to one another*, be kind to people who have less than you. Don't think bad things about each other.' But the people ignored God and did all those evil things so he punished them – he allowed their enemies to take them into *exile*."

5. "God also blamed the Israelite leaders who led the people away from him. He said, 'I want my people to love me. *I will restore them because I have compassion on them.*[84] Once again the city of Jerusalem will be a place of peace and enjoyment – that's tough for you to imagine now, but it's not hard for me, because I am God! People from all over the world will come to Jerusalem to seek God and speak to him. *Do not be afraid, but let your hands be strong*[85] to obey me.'"

6. "But God's enemies who attack his people will be burnt up by fire. God's *arrow will flash like lightning* and *he will march in the storms*."[86]

---

81. Zechariah 1:3.
82. Zechariah 3:2.
83 Zechariah 3:4.
84. Zechariah 10:6.
85. Zechariah 8:13.
86. Zechariah 9:14.

LEARNING FROM ZECHARIAH

1. God has removed sin from people through all of history, and one day he will remove it from his people forever. He will bring the peace and *salvation* they have waited for so long, while they suffered many difficulties (See overview paragraphs 2–3 and 5).

   Bible references: Zechariah 3:4-5, 9; Leviticus 16:30; Hebrews 9:28.

   Questions: How would it feel to be really dirty from playing outside and then get into a clean bed without washing? It wouldn't feel good, and it would spoil the sheets. God cleans us from our sin before we go to heaven, so that heaven can really be heaven – no sin, but a perfect place!

2. The *Israelites* weren't building the *temple* as God told them to, and they started to treat people badly. But they would *fast* because they thought it would keep God happy with them. Going to church or reading our Bibles doesn't mean that we can treat people badly or disobey God in other ways (See overview paragraphs 4–5).

   Bible references: Zechariah 7:5-6, 9-10; Deuteronomy 27:19; James 1:27.

   Questions: If you saw someone stealing but they said it didn't matter because they loved God, what would you think?

3. God will punish those who make themselves his enemies and refuse to worship him (See overview paragraphs 1 and 6).

   Bible references: Zechariah 12:9; Leviticus 26:21; 2 Timothy 4:14-15.

   Questions: Why do people refuse to worship God? Why should we worship God?

SALVATION THREAD

Sixty-seven times in the New Testament, something was written that goes back to the prophecy of Zechariah. For example:

1. "Rejoice greatly, O daughter of Zion! … See, your king comes to you, righteous and having salvation, gentle and riding on a donkey, on a colt, the foal of a donkey" (Zechariah 9:9).

   "Say to the daughter of Zion, 'See, your king comes to you, gentle and riding on a donkey, on a colt, the foal of a donkey'" (Matthew 21:5).

   Jesus entered Jerusalem riding on a donkey, less than a week before he was crucified. At that time many people treated him like a king (which he is!).

2. "Strike the shepherd, and the sheep will be scattered, and I will turn my hand against the little ones" (Zechariah 13:7).

   Then Jesus told them, "This very night you will all fall away on account of me, for it is written: 'I will strike the shepherd, and the sheep of the flock will be scattered'" (Matthew 26:31).

   After Jesus was arrested, all the disciples ran away because they were scared of what might happen to them.

Key Verse: "Rejoice greatly, O Daughter of Zion! Shout, Daughter of Jerusalem! See, your king comes to you, righteous and having salvation …" (Zechariah 9:9).

The book of
MALACHI

MALACHI

'My messenger'[87]

INTRODUCTION

- Will the people never learn? A thousand years of disobedience to God resulted in defeat by Israel's enemies and being taken into *exile*. But even when God brought them back from *exile*, his people still did not love and worship him as they should. They were discouraged because the country they went back to was much smaller than before – other countries had captured their land.

- Malachi was the last prophet of the Old Testament. He was God's last big call to his people before everything seemed to go silent from God for over 400 years, until John the Baptist, then the arrival of Jesus as a baby.

- Malachi probably prophesied some time around 450 B.C.

OVERVIEW

1. "'*I have loved you*[88] ahead of other nations,' says God to Israel. 'Edom says they will rebuild their ruins, but they will be forever punished for their wickedness.'"

2. "'You *Israelites* have disrespected me with bad sacrifices. I would rather you didn't offer sacrifices at all – I will not accept them. You don't even want to offer them. You priests should speak knowledge. People should want to learn from you because your job is to be God's messengers, but you have broken promises and led people away from God instead.'"

3. "'Why are God's people unfaithful to their wives and to me?' God says. God is tired of people being unfaithful; they love evil and think that God does nothing about it. '*See, I will send my messenger, who will prepare the way before me. Then suddenly the LORD you are seeking will come to his temple; the messenger of the covenant, whom you desire, will come,' says the LORD Almighty.*[94] He will get rid of evil and leave only good."

4. "God said, 'I will judge those who treat people badly and have no respect for me. *Return to me, and I will return to you.*[89] I am ready to give you great blessings yet you refuse to bring the offerings you promised. You even said, "It is pointless to serve God – it got us nowhere. Evil people have better lives."'"

5. "*Surely the day is coming; it will burn like a furnace. All the arrogant and every evildoer will be stubble*[90] ... and nothing will be left. But those who worship God will have blessing, and victory over the wicked. '*Remember the law of my servant Moses*

---

87. Malachi means, 'my messenger', meaning the messenger from God.
88. Malachi 1:2.
89. Malachi 3:7.
90. Malachi 4:1.

... See I will send you the prophet Elijah before that great and dreadful day of the LORD *comes.'"*[91]

LEARNING FROM MALACHI

1. The *Israelites* knew they had to offer sacrifices to God, but they didn't really want to give him anything good, so they just offered bad sacrifices and thought that would be okay. If we can't be bothered to obey God, but just want to look like we do, then we are like those Israelites (See overview paragraph 2).

    Bible references: Malachi 1:7-8, 13; Genesis 4:3-7; Romans 12:1-2.

    Questions: What can you give to God that will cost you? Time? Money? Talents? How might someone pretend to love God?

2. It is important to keep promises. God was sad to see so many husbands leave their wives, breaking their promise to stay with them. The *Israelites* also broke other promises to God. We must pray to follow the example of God who always keeps his promises (See overview paragraph 2).

    Bible references: Malachi 2:10-11, 14; Joshua 21:45; Romans 15:8-9.

    Question: What are some of God's promises? What would it be like if God broke his promises?

3. Many *Israelites* thought that God either wasn't doing anything, didn't care what they did, or couldn't do anything about it. Don't make the same mistake. God will punish *sin*, and he will bless his people (See overview paragraphs 3–5).

    Bible references: Malachi 2:17; 3:18; Habakkuk 2:3; Romans 2:4.

    Questions: Does God do anything about our sin? Does he care about it? (Think about what Jesus did).

SALVATION THREAD

Through Malachi, God said: "See, I will send my messenger, who will prepare the way before me. Then suddenly the Lord you are seeking will come to his temple; the messenger of the covenant, who you desire, will come" (Malachi 3:1).

Malachi and Isaiah both prophesied in this way about John the Baptist, and Matthew wrote about it in his gospel (Matthew 3:1-3). John the Baptist prepared the way for Jesus by saying that Jesus was coming soon, and he told people they needed to repent.

Malachi 3:1 tells us about the "messenger" (John the Baptist) but also about the "Lord" and "messenger of the *covenant*" who would come after him. That man is Jesus, "whom you desire" because he would come to save his people from their sins. It was hundreds of years after Malachi when John the Baptist and Jesus came, but God sent them at just the right time, keeping his promises to his people just as he keeps his promises to us.

Key Verse: "... you will again see the distinction between the righteous and the wicked, between those who serve God and those who do not" (Malachi 3:18).

---

91. Malachi 4:4-5.

165

GOSPELS AND ACTS

The book of
MATTHEW

MATTHEW

The promised Messiah has come

INTRODUCTION

- Everybody hated tax collectors. They took too much money from people and worked for the *Romans*. Matthew was a tax collector and yet, amazingly, Jesus chose him to be one of his twelve special followers, called *disciples*! Matthew spent three years with Jesus. He wrote this book because he wanted people to understand that Jesus is the *Messiah*, who God had promised would be sent to save his people.

- Matthew wrote the gospel some time between A.D. 57 and 63, about events from 6 B.C. to A.D. 70.

OVERVIEW

1. "Jesus, the *Messiah*, is Jewish. His family tree goes back to Abraham, Isaac and Jacob. When Jesus was born to his mother Mary, King Herod was jealous and killed all the baby boys in Bethlehem to try and kill Jesus. However, Jesus' family escaped to Egypt. This happened to fulfill what God said through the prophets would happen."

2. "When Jesus was grown up, he went into the desert for forty days and was tempted by *Satan*. Jesus resisted Satan and said, '*You shall not put the Lord your God to the test.*'"[92]

3. "Jesus taught people how to live well, including loving others, even if they hate you. He said, '... *in everything, do to others what you would have them do to you, for this sums up the Law and the Prophets.*'[93] Jesus fulfilled *prophecy* by healing many people. He cast out demons, raised people from the dead, and did many other miracles."

4. "Jesus preached that people should *repent* and follow him. He also told parables. In one he said that the Kingdom of *heaven* is like treasure that you would do anything to get because it's most precious."

5. "Jesus told his *disciples* three times that he would be killed by the religious leaders, and then rise from the dead, but they didn't understand him. Judas Iscariot betrayed Jesus to the religious leaders in return for money. They arrested Jesus, and when they asked him, '*Are you the Son of God?*' he said, 'Yes'. This made them even more determined to kill him. The Roman ruler[94] let that happen, even though he knew they only wanted to kill Jesus because they were jealous that the people wanted to listen to him instead of them."

---

92. Matthew 4:7; Deuteronomy 6:16.
93. Matthew 7:12.
94. The Romans were in charge of the country because they invaded Israel and defeated them in war.

6. "Jesus rose from the dead after three days, just as he said he would. Before he went back to *heaven*, he told his *disciples* to teach people everywhere about him. He promised, '*I am with you always, to the very end of the age.*'⁹⁵

LEARNING FROM MATTHEW

1. God's words and prophecies are true; he keeps his promises. God's biggest promise and prophecy was that he would send a Messiah to save his people (See overview paragraphs 1, 3, 5–6).

   Bible references: Genesis 3:15; 1 Kings 8:24; Matthew 1:18-23; 2:15; Acts 13:27-29.

   Question: Which promises and prophecies by God the Father and Jesus can we see came true in the book of Matthew? Is it important that we know God keeps all his promises? Why?

2. King Herod and the religious leaders were jealous of Jesus because they didn't want anyone to be more important than them. But Jesus is the king, so we should worship him and ask him to lead us (See overview paragraphs 1 and 5).

   Bible references: Matthew 2:1-3; 27:17-18; Isaiah 45:23; Acts 17:2-5.

   Question: Do you want Jesus to be the king of your life, or do you want to be in charge yourself?

3. Jesus taught that we should love everybody, which means being kind and treating everyone in the same way we would like them to treat us. Not just people who like us or who are our friends, but also people who don't like us, or who do nasty things (See overview paragraph 3).

   Bible references: Matthew 5:43-44; Proverbs 17:9; John 13:34-35.

   Question: How do you feel about people when they do or say bad things to you? Do you sometimes want to be nasty right back at them?

SALVATION THREAD

Matthew was a Jew, and was taught about God from when he was a child. The Jews looked forward to the time when the *Messiah* would arrive to save his people. Like the other *disciples*, Matthew didn't fully understand that Jesus was the *Messiah*, until after Jesus rose from the dead. Once he understood, he wanted everyone else to understand it. Matthew wanted Jews especially to know that everything written in the Bible (our Old Testament) pointed to Jesus, and that what happened in Jesus' life was what the prophets in the Old Testament said would happen. Those prophecies were God's promises.

One of the prophecies about the *Messiah* was that he would come from the family line of King David⁹⁶ – he would be a "Son of David". Matthew includes examples of people calling Jesus that (e.g. chapter 9:27), to show that people were beginning to understand who Jesus is.

It's important for people of all nationalities to know that Jesus was a real man from a real family. The Bible shows us. And Jesus proved that he was the *Messiah* by doing and being everything that God promised the *Messiah* would do and be. So we can trust him. Thank God that he keeps all his promises. Thank God that the *Messiah* of the Jews was and is also the Savior for people everywhere who *repent*.

Key Verse: "But this has all taken place that the writings of the prophets might be fulfilled" (Matthew 26:56).

---

95. Matthew 28:20.
96. e.g. Jeremiah 23:5-6.

The book of

MARK

MARK

The beginning of the good news about Jesus

INTRODUCTION

- What would it be like if two of the most amazing Christians ever were good friends with you? Mark knew, because he was a good friend of Peter and Paul. Mark's missionary life started badly when he abandoned Paul and Barnabas but later, Mark became helpful to Paul. The gospel that Mark wrote probably used a lot of information from Peter's preaching, and was mainly for Gentile readers who lived in Rome.

- Mark wrote the gospel between A.D. 55 and 59, about events from 6 B.C. to A.D. 70.

OVERVIEW

1. "John the Baptist made people ready for Jesus, preaching that everyone should repent and have their sins forgiven. Jesus preached the same thing."

2. "Jesus healed people, made evil spirits come out of people, and forgave people their sins. Some of those he helped had done many bad things, so the religious leaders said Jesus shouldn't spend time with them."

3. "Jesus taught using parables. One was about a farmer sowing seed: most fell on places where seed didn't grow. This is like people who hear God's Word but don't obey it. But some seed fell on good soil and grew well. This is like people who hear and obey God's Word. God makes them more like Jesus."

4. "The religious leaders complained that Jesus didn't keep all the Jewish traditions. Jesus told them, 'You are more interested in making your own rules than keeping God's rules.' He told his *disciples*, 'People will hurt you and put you in prison when you tell them about me. But the Holy Spirit will give you the best words to say when this happens.'"

5. "Many people did not understand who Jesus was. Some thought he was a prophet or another good man from God. Jesus asked Peter what he thought, and Peter said, '*You are the Christ.*'"[97]

6. "Five days before Jesus died, he finished his long walk to Jerusalem. Crowds of people were happy to see him. Next day, Monday, he cleared the *temple* of people who tried to make money from those who were simply there to worship God. On Thursday Jesus was arrested and taken for trial. People lied about what Jesus had done and said, and he was sentenced to death."

---

97. Mark 8:29.

7. "On Friday, Roman soldiers nailed Jesus to a cross of wood, where he died. On Sunday he rose to life. An angel appeared to two women at the tomb, and told them that Jesus was alive again, just as he said he would be."

LEARNING FROM MARK

1. The main message in the preaching of John the Baptist, and Jesus, and also his *disciples,* was that people should *repent,* and then their sins would be forgiven. God gives that same message to us today. If we *repent,* our sins are forgiven. We do not need to worry that God will punish us, because Jesus has taken our punishment through his death on the *cross* (See overview paragraph 1).

   Bible references: Mark 1:4, 15; 6:12; Ezekiel 14:6; Acts 3:19; Romans 8:1; 1 John 1:9.
   Questions: Have you obeyed God by repenting of your sins? Do you trust God that those sins really are forgiven, or do you still worry about them?

2. Jesus suffered because people didn't like what he said. We too will suffer if we love and obey Jesus. Sometimes people won't like what we say, and they will do or say bad things to us (See overview paragraphs 4, 6 and 7).

   Bible references: Mark 8:34-38; 13:9-13; Nehemiah 2:18-19; John 15:18.
   Question: Has anyone ever laughed or said bad things to you because you have spoken to them about the Bible, or about Jesus?

3. It is important to know who Jesus is. Mark helps us to understand that he is God, that he is a man, and that he was the promised one from God the Father (See overview paragraph 5).

   Bible references: Mark 8:27-29; Acts 17:2-4; 1 Timothy 2:5.
   Question: Who do you think Jesus is? Why?

SALVATION THREAD

When Mark was in Rome with Peter after Jesus went back to heaven, Christians were a tiny and unpopular group.

Mark helped them, and helps us, to understand that the story of Jesus is real history. He included lots of details, for example about a man who had a devil in him. "Night and day among the tombs and in the hills he would cry out and cut himself with stones," Mark wrote.[98] Most writers didn't bother with details like that, especially when they were making things up. Mark wanted everyone to know that this all really happened.

Mark also wanted to make sure people knew that Jesus was who he said he was: God and man. He pointed out that even devils know this (see Mark 3:11 and 5:7). He gave other examples of people like Peter, who knew Jesus day-to-day and also believed he was God (Mark 8:29).

Mark also tells about people who didn't believe in Jesus (Mark 3:22), and the terrible things they did to Jesus. After the Christians in Rome read that, it wasn't a surprise when people treated them badly for being Christians.

Key Verse: "Love the Lord your God with all your heart and with all your soul and with all your mind and with all your strength" (Mark 12:30).

---

98. Mark 5:5.

The book of
LUKE

LUKE

The number one history book for everyone, forever

INTRODUCTION

- The story of Jesus is the most important story ever. Luke wanted to make sure people got it right. Some made-up stories had been going around and Luke wanted Theophilus and others to know the truth. He wrote his book after talking to the apostles and other people who knew Jesus while he was on earth. Luke was a doctor and one of Paul the apostle's most loyal friends.

- Luke wrote the gospel between A.D. 62 and 64, about events from 6 B.C. to A.D. 70.

OVERVIEW

1. "Theophilus, I have carefully investigated everything about Jesus and am writing this so that you can know for sure that what you were taught about Jesus is true."

2. "The angel Gabriel came to a young lady called Mary who was not married and had not been with a man. He said, '*You will … give birth to a son, and you are to give him the name Jesus.*'[99] This came true just as Gabriel said."

3. "Jesus grew up, and while John the Baptist was baptizing him, the Holy Spirit came down on Jesus in the form of a dove. God the Father spoke from *heaven* and said to Jesus: '*You are my Son, whom I love; with you I am well pleased.*'[100] John preached that people needed to *repent*, and obey God, and that just because they were from Israel did not mean they were right with God."

4. "Jesus traveled from town to town, preaching about the Kingdom of God. He showed what that kingdom was like by healing people, including the servant of a Roman soldier who, Jesus said, had more *faith* than the people of Israel. The religious leaders thought they didn't need *faith*, but Jesus said they did. He said they were like sick people who didn't want to see a doctor, and told them, 'You have made it difficult for people to know God'. Jesus then said to the *disciples*, 'People from all over the world will love me and go to *heaven*, but many others will hate you because they hate me – I will be killed and then rise again to life three days later.'"

5. "Eventually the religious leaders arrested Jesus, and after he said that he was the Son of God they made definite plans to kill him. When Jesus was put on the *cross* to die, criminals were put on crosses either side of him. One of them insulted Jesus, the other defended Jesus, and asked Jesus to remember him. Jesus replied, '*I tell you the truth, today you will be with me in paradise.*'[101] "Jesus died, and then he came alive

99. Luke 1:31.
100. Luke 3:22.
101. Luke 23:43.

from the dead three days later. He appeared to over 500 people, and then went back to heaven."

LEARNING FROM LUKE

1. The good news of forgiveness is for everyone: Jews and Gentiles, nice people and nasty people, men and women, girls and boys, rich and poor. Jesus showed this when he healed a Roman's servant, spent time with children and forgave a criminal (See overview paragraphs 3–5).

   Bible references: Luke 2:30-32; Numbers 10:29-32; Romans 1:16.

   Questions: Who do you think is more different to you than anyone else? (Maybe they talk differently or like different things?). Does God love one of you more than the other one?

2. Jesus being alive on earth, and when he rejected, killed, but then rose from the dead, was all part of God's plan to save his people (See overview paragraphs 2 and 4).

   Bible references: Luke 4:43; 9:22; Isaiah 14:24; Ephesians 1:11.

   Question: If everything is part of God's plan, can we trust God to do as he promises? Do you trust him?

3. Luke wrote this gospel so that people could be sure that what they had heard about Jesus was true. You too can trust what the gospels say about Jesus because it all really happened (See overview paragraph 1).

   Bible references: Luke 1:1-4; Psalm 119:160; 2 Timothy 3:16.

   Questions: How would you feel about walking on a frozen lake? Probably very nervous, in case you fell through the ice into the freezing water. Do you feel too nervous to trust Jesus, because you wonder whether it is all true? That is why Luke wrote this book, so that people could know that what Jesus said, what he did, and what happened to him, was all real.

SALVATION THREAD

The Jews were chosen by God to be his special people. Jesus was a Jew, and the first missionary to the Gentiles – Paul the *apostle* – was a Jew. Every book in the Old Testament was written by a Jew. So when we get to Luke (and Luke's other book in the Bible called Acts) it's different – Luke was a *Gentile* not a Jew. His two books are the only two books of the Bible written by a *Gentile*. They are like a big exclamation mark from God saying, 'Yes! The *gospel* is for ALL people!'

All through history there were little moments where people could see that forgiveness of sins was for everyone. For example, God told Abraham that his family would be a blessing to all nations (Genesis 18:18), Gentiles joined God's people when they went to the *promised land* (Exodus 12:48-49) and there were Gentiles in Jesus' family line (e.g. Ruth).

But most Jews still didn't understand it, even after Jesus came. After Jesus went back to heaven, the apostles obeyed Jesus by taking the message to other countries (Ephesians 3:6).

Key Verse: "Jesus answered them, 'It is not the healthy who need a doctor, but the sick. I have not come to call the righteous, but sinners to repentance'" (Luke 5:31).

The book of
JOHN

JOHN

The way, the truth and the life has come to earth

INTRODUCTION

- John was one of the twelve *disciples*, and most of his best friends were killed for being Christians. By the time he wrote his book – 40-70 years after Jesus went back to heaven – John was an old man. He wanted to help people understand that Jesus was the promised *Messiah* and truly God.
- John wrote the gospel some time between A.D. 70 and 100, about events from 6 B.C. to A.D. 96.

OVERVIEW

1. "Jesus was always with God, and he is God forever. Everything was made through Jesus, and in him is life. John the Baptist was sent by God to tell people about Jesus, so that people would believe in him."

2. "One day when Jesus was walking through a region called Samaria, he spoke to a woman and showed her that he is the *Messiah*. She told lots of people, who came to Jesus and believed in him. Jesus told people about himself, saying things like, '*I and the Father are one*,'[102] '*I am the bread of life*,'[103] the '*light of the world*'[104] and '*the way, the truth and the life*.'[105] 'The only way to get to God the Father is through me,' he said."

3. "He raised a man called Lazarus from the dead, and many Jews put their *faith* in him. However, some leaders were afraid that if Jesus became too popular the *Romans* would become even stricter with them, so they decided to kill Jesus. Other people thought Jesus was crazy, or possessed by the devil."

4. "'I have chosen you and will keep you safe with me forever,' Jesus told his *disciples*. 'The Holy Spirit will tell people about me, and you also must tell people about me.'"

5. "Later, the religious leaders arrested Jesus. Crowds of people shouted for him to be killed because he claimed to be God. The Roman ruler gave in to them, and had Jesus nailed to a *cross* to kill him. While he was on the cross, Jesus said, '*It is finished*,'[106] and then allowed himself to die. After Jesus rose from the dead, he appeared to Mary Magdalene and to the *disciples*, who finally understood from the Bible that Jesus had to die and then rise again."

---

102. John 10:30.
103. John 6:35.
104. John 8:12.
105. John 14:6
106. John 19:30

6. "Jesus did many miracles, but I have written these ones down so *that you may believe that Jesus is the Christ, the Son of God, and that by believing you may have life in his name.*"[107]

LEARNING FROM JOHN

1. Jesus is the greatest man, and he is God – the *Messiah*, the Son of God. He proved this by all the miracles he did. Because Jesus is God and man, his death on the cross means that we can be forgiven for our sins (See overview paragraphs 1–3 and 5–6).

   Bible references: John 20:31; Acts 2:22; Hebrews 10:10; 1 John 4:10.

   Question: John the Baptist preached, and Jesus preached and did miracles, for the same reason. What was that?

2. People have different ideas about Jesus. Some don't like him, some think what he said was nonsense, and some think he is just a man. Other people understand and believe that Jesus is God (See overview paragraphs 1–3 and 5–6).

   Bible references: John 12:12-13; 19:6-7; Hosea 13:14; 1 John 4:3.

   Questions: Who do you think Jesus is?

3. To beat sin, Jesus had to beat death. He did that, and proved it when he showed himself to many people after he rose from the dead (See overview paragraph 5).

   Bible references: John 20:10–21:14; Acts 1:3; 2:24; 1 Corinthians 15:3-8.

   Question: Over five thousand people saw Jesus after he rose, and many of them were killed because they refused to lie and say it wasn't true. Do you believe that he rose from the dead? Why or why not?

SALVATION THREAD

Everything that comes before the gospels – the whole of the Old Testament – leads up to the coming of Jesus.

Matthew, Mark and Luke gave the story about Jesus' life. John didn't give so much of the story, but concentrated on the miracles. They help us understand that Jesus is God, and that we can have eternal life if we believe in him. John also wrote more of Jesus' teaching than the other gospels. For example, Jesus taught about how he and God the Father are together and united[108] That if people want to know God the Father they must love and obey Jesus.[109]

Key Verse: "For God so loved the world that he gave his one and only Son, that whoever believes in him shall not perish but have eternal life … whoever does not believe stands condemned already because he has not believed in the name of God's one and only Son" (John 3:16-18).

---

107. John 20:31.
108. John 10:30.
109. John 14:6-7, 15.

The book of
ACTS

ACTS

What Jesus did next: the good news spreads

INTRODUCTION

- Luke was shipwrecked, and he witnessed riots and miracles. He saw people believing in Jesus, and people trying to worship Paul one moment and kill him the next. Those events were a result of the apostles, who obeyed Jesus and spread the good news of the gospel. Some people accepted the good news, others tried to stop it. Luke wrote Acts to tell that story, and was the second book[110] he wrote for a man called Theophilus.[111] It is an introduction to the rest of the New Testament, which is mainly letters written by the apostles Paul, Peter and John, who are all in this book.

- Acts is written about events from about A.D. 30 to 67.

OVERVIEW

1. "Soon after Jesus went back to *heaven*, the Holy Spirit came down on the *disciples* while they were together in Jerusalem. Suddenly they were able to speak in foreign languages, and told the gospel to people who were in Jerusalem from all over the world. 3,000 believed in Jesus in one day, and the *disciples* continued to teach and do miracles."

2. "Later, when Peter and John were arrested, the religious leaders said they must stop telling people about Jesus. But Peter and John said, '*we cannot help speaking about what we have seen and heard.*'[112] After a *Christian* called Stephen was killed, many Jewish leaders in Jerusalem started to *persecute* the Christians, who ran away to different parts of the country, where they kept telling people about Jesus."

3. "Paul (while he was still called Saul) was a *Pharisee* who *persecuted* Christians. However, one day Jesus showed him that he (Jesus) really is God. God told him to take the *gospel* to the Gentiles. Some Jews kept trying to kill Paul because they were jealous of the Gentiles. They thought that God loved only the Jews."

4. "Paul was put in prison many times. He was beaten, whipped and injured. But he kept telling people about Jesus. He healed people, set up churches and encouraged Christians to keep on loving Jesus. Paul went on long journeys to different countries to do this. At a big meeting with Jewish *Christian* leaders, Paul showed them that God wanted the Gentiles to hear the *gospel*, so that they also could believe and be saved as a free gift from God. Gentiles did not have to do anything extra to be like the Jews."

5. "But that seemed wrong to many Jews who had not become Christians, so when Paul went back to Jerusalem, he was arrested again. The Roman rulers could see he had not done anything wrong, but kept him in prison for years to please the Jewish

---

110. The first book is called Luke – named after the author. It is the third book in the New Testament.
111. Theophilus was a man, probably from Rome.
112. Acts 4:20.

religious leaders. Then Paul was taken to Rome to go on trial. He kept on preaching about God and Jesus on the way, even when he was shipwrecked. And when he was taken to prison in Rome he still told people about Jesus."

LEARNING FROM ACTS

1. God does amazing things through the Holy Spirit. Jesus promised his *disciples* that he would send the Holy Spirit to help them teach people about Jesus (See overview paragraph 1).

   Bible references: Acts 1:4-5; Joel 2:28-32; John 15:26.

   Questions: What happened when the Holy Spirit was given to the disciples? How did he help people to know about Jesus?

2. Many people don't like the good news of God's free gift of forgiveness. Some people think the free gift is only for them, or that other people don't deserve it, or should earn it in some way. Some of the Jews were jealous, so they tried to stop the Christians from sharing the *gospel* with people they didn't like, especially the Gentiles (See overview paragraphs 3–5).

   Bible references: Acts 17:2-5; Matthew 27:17-18.

   Questions: What did people do to try and stop Peter, John and Paul telling people about Jesus? Did they succeed? Who do you think the *gospel* is for?

3. God does not let the good news about Jesus be silenced. It was first preached in Jerusalem, then it spread to other parts of Israel, and on to other countries in Europe, Africa and Asia. Now it is all over the world (See overview paragraphs 1–5).

   Bible references: Acts 1:8; Isaiah 49:6; Colossians 1:6.

   Question: What are three ways in which the gospel started to spread?[113] Find your country on a map, and then find Israel and its capital city Jerusalem. See how far the gospel had to go from Jerusalem before it reached you.

SALVATION THREAD

God's promises to his people from the Old Testament keep coming true in Acts, after Jesus went back to *heaven*. Joel prophesied about the Holy Spirit in chapter 2:28-32 of his book. Jesus also promised the Holy Spirit to his *disciples* and it's no surprise that it was true – just like all God's other promises. When the *disciples* spoke in different languages, many people who heard the *gospel* took it back to their countries, which God promised would happen (see Isaiah 49:6).

Luke also showed that Jesus' story goes on forever. Read chapter 1 verse 1 – he wrote about the things that Jesus "began" to do while he was on earth. Matthew, Mark, Luke and John were not the end of the story about God bringing his people to himself. They were simply the end of one part of the story, and the beginning of the next part.

Key Verse: "The word of the Lord spread through the whole region ... And the disciples were filled with joy and with the Holy Spirit" (Acts 13:49, 52).

---

113. a.) The people in Jerusalem who went there from all over the world and then heard the gospel in their own language eventually went home, and told people back home about Jesus. b.) When the Christians ran away because of persecution, they began to tell people in different parts of Israel about Jesus. c.) Paul traveled around Europe and Asia to share the gospel.

EPISTLES

The book of

ROMANS

ROMANS

God's great justice and mercy is revealed

INTRODUCTION

- Paul the *apostle* wanted to take the good news about Jesus to Spain. On his way he planned to stay in Rome, and wrote to the Christians there to say he hoped to be with them soon. First he had to take some much needed money to the church in Jerusalem. He wanted the Jewish and *Gentile* Christians in Rome to understand the *gospel* of Jesus, and how that fit with what God said in the Old Testament.

- Paul wrote this letter in about A.D. 57.

OVERVIEW

1. Paul wrote, "*Paul, a servant of Christ Jesus, called to be an apostle and set apart for the gospel of God – the gospel he promised beforehand through his prophets in the Holy Scriptures regarding his Son, who ... was a descendant of David, and ... the Son of God ...*"[114]

2. "I am proud of the gospel, because it is the power of God, saving people from sin. God's anger and punishment is against those who refuse to believe in God – foolish people who care more about things that are made, than the one who made them. But God is willing to forgive, and make *holy*, all those who believe in him and trust in Jesus. Remember, even the great man Abraham wasn't saved because he did good things, but because he believed in God, who gave him the gift of forgiveness and made him *holy*."

3. "*Sin* came into the world through Adam. God's free gift of forgiveness came through Jesus. Now that Jesus has been punished for our sins and God has made us free from *sin*, let's stop sinning! We should hate *sin* and love other people."

4. "The law can't save us because we can't keep it – that's why Jesus came to earth, paying the price for our sin so we can be saved. The whole of creation – including God's people – is going to be made new again by God, and we wait patiently for that. Who can accuse us of anything if God has made us right with him? No-one! Nothing and no-one can separate us from God's love, not even death."

5. "What makes me sad is that so many *Israelites* don't accept Jesus. However, I know that all God's chosen people from all countries will come to God. That includes many *Israelites*, and it's up to God how he does it."

---

114. Romans 1:1-4.

6. *"If you confess with your mouth, 'Jesus is Lord', and believe in your heart that God raised him from the dead, you will be saved ...*[115] – it's the same for Jews and Gentiles. I really want to take that good news about Jesus to people who haven't heard it. Hopefully, I'll do that in Spain after I've visited you."

LEARNING FROM ROMANS

1. God punishes those who reject him and choose sin instead, but he forgives those who believe in him and ask to be forgiven. There are only two possibilities: rejecting God or trusting him (See overview paragraph 2).

    Bible references: Romans 3:22-24; Hosea 4:6; Hebrews 10:39.

    Question: God says sin is real and causes death. How do you feel about sin?

2. God will bring people from all over the world, and all kinds of places, into his kingdom (See overview paragraph 1–2, 5–6).

    Bible references: Romans 1:5, 8; 4:17; Genesis 17:5; Acts 9:15.

    Questions: What did Paul write about the gospel of Jesus? What did he want to do with it? Why?

3. There is nothing we can do to save ourselves, so don't try! Instead, thank God that he gives us forgiveness, and makes us right with him even though we don't deserve it. The Christians in Rome were tempted to try and save themselves, and sometimes we might think if we do enough good things, God will save us (See overview paragraphs 2 and 4).

    Bible references: Romans 10:3-4; 15:9-12; Isaiah 25:9; Galatians 3:23.

    Questions: How good do you think you need to be to deserve *heaven*? Can you do that? What does God say that we must do to be saved?

SALVATION THREAD

"For if, by the trespass [*sin*] of the one man, death reigned through that one man, how much more will those who receive God's abundant provision of *grace* and of the gift of righteousness reign in life through the one man, Jesus Christ" (Romans 5:17).

Romans reminds us that the Bible is one big story. Paul the *apostle* wrote about how *sin* came into the world through Adam when he and Eve ate the fruit from the one tree that God told them not to ("the trespass of the one man"). When *sin* came into the world, death came with it and has been here ever since. However, Jesus ("promised beforehand through [God's] prophets") came into the world, He brought life with him. That life that comes through forgiveness and *righteousness* from God.

Key Verse: "... I am not ashamed of the *gospel*, because it is the power of God that brings *salvation* to everyone who believes: first to the Jew, then to the *Gentile*" (Romans 1:16).

---

115. Romans 10:9.

The books of
1 & 2 CORINTHIANS

1 CORINTHIANS

Learning to love God in a godless place

INTRODUCTION

- The Corinthians badly misunderstood Paul's previous letter (which isn't in the Bible). They disobeyed God in terrible ways and thought too much of themselves. Corinth was a big city in Greece with twelve temples to false gods. The church there was young and they found it difficult to obey God.

- Paul wrote this letter in either A.D. 53, 54 or 55.

OVERVIEW

1. "From Paul and Sosthenes to Christians in Corinth and everywhere. I thank God for all that he's done for you and what he has made you good at."

2. "I ask that you stop all arguments about which teacher you like best – you are focusing on the wrong thing. While I was with you I focused totally on the true message of Jesus and what he did on the cross. That is the message that has power, even though lots of people don't like it and don't believe it."

3. "So don't boast about other people, or yourselves. Everything you have is from God, and not because you are better than anyone else. You should think like me – I know that telling people about Jesus is more important than people thinking I'm really good."

4. "It is important that you live in the way Jesus wants you to. Jesus' death took away your *sin*, which means that you can go to *heaven*. So you should want to stay away from *sin*."

5. "Now to answer a couple of your questions. Some people want to get married, which is okay. Some don't want to get married which gives them more opportunity to do things for God and that's great. When you have married someone you must stay married and not leave them."

6. "Everything we do should be for God and to help other people know God better. That includes being kind to each other, and doing what you are good at to help each other. All of this should be because you love God and love people."

7. "Remember what I told you and keep hold of it: Jesus died for our sins and came to life again. This is most important."

LEARNING FROM 1 CORINTHIANS

1. When Jesus died on the cross, it meant that he was punished for sins. Not his own sins, because he was perfect. He was punished for the sins of everyone who says yes to God's free gift of forgiveness. Saying yes to that means really being sorry for our sins, and if we are really sorry for our sins then we don't want to do them any more (See overview paragraph 4).

   Bible references: 1 Corinthians 6:9-11; Leviticus 16:9-10; Romans 6:1-2.

   Question: Have you asked God to help you to want to obey him? He promises that he will help us with that if we ask him.

2. Think about Jesus and what he did when he died on the cross and rose again (See overview paragraphs 2–3 and 7).

   Bible references: 1 Corinthians 2:2; Psalm 63:6; Acts 4:18-20.

   Question: Lots of people don't like to hear about Jesus. Does that mean we should stop talking about him? Why?

3. One person is not more important than another (See overview paragraphs 2–3).

   Bible references: 1 Corinthians 4:7; 12:13; Psalm 94:4; Romans 12:3.

   Questions: What do people boast about? Do any of those things make them better than other people?

SALVATION THREAD

Living as a *Christian* is not easy because it means living in a different way to most people. The Corinthians were too interested in getting their own way or looking cool. They behaved in whatever way they wanted, and argued in order to get their own way. They took each other to court. They were more interested in which preacher they liked best rather than following God. Paul told them that was against what Jesus taught,[116] and they needed to live differently.

Through 1 Corinthians we are reminded that being a *Christian* isn't just about saying you believe something, it is about how you live. That is because if we really love Jesus and have repented of our sins, then we won't want to *sin* any more.[117] God calls his people out of the ways of the world, to live as his special, *holy* people. The Christians in Corinth lived in a place full of wicked living, and they struggled to break away from that. It is tempting for us if we are Christians just to live like everyone else. We need to ask God to help us not to just say that we love God, but to live like it as well.

Key Verse: "Be on your guard; stand firm in the *faith*; be men of courage; be strong. Do everything in love" (1 Corinthians 16:13-14).

---

116. 1 Corinthians 3:1-4.
117. John 14:15.

2 CORINTHIANS

Paul defends his ministry against attacks

INTRODUCTION

- These people were hard work! About a year after writing 1 Corinthians Paul had to write again. False teachers lied about Paul and about the *gospel*, and influenced some people in the church. If the Corinthians believed the lies about Paul, they might also think his message about Jesus was wrong. So he wanted to make sure they understood that he was living for God and doing right things for the *gospel*.

- Paul wrote this letter around A.D. 55/56.

OVERVIEW

1. "From Paul and Timothy to the Christians in and near the city of Corinth."

2. "I have decided to make one long visit to you instead of the two shorter visits I planned at first. It's okay that I changed my mind about this, and doesn't mean I might change my mind on what I told you about Jesus."

3. "God has given me this wonderful message of new life with Jesus to tell everyone. I don't change it when I tell it to you. Even when people don't like it, I don't change it, because it is true. It is difficult sometimes to keep going with my work but I look forward to being with God forever and that helps me carry on. I think about *heaven* and how awesome and amazing God is, and it makes me want to tell people about Jesus even more."

4. "I love you very much and I wish that you would love me back."

5. "You are very good at lots of things and it would be great if you could be good at giving people things. Giving to other people means that God will give you more to give away. For example, Christians in Jerusalem urgently need money for food so please make sure you send them what you promised."

6. "Some people have said bad things about me and about the message of Jesus, but what they say doesn't make sense. Some of them boast that they are better Christians than me. They're not. And anyway, you should boast about how great God is, not about how great you think you are. You need to be careful and not just believe everything that anyone tells you."

7. "Finally, make sure that you are living as Christians should live so that when I visit you it will be nice for you and I won't have to be angry."

LEARNING FROM 2 CORINTHIANS

1. When we tell people about Jesus we should be careful to say only what the Bible says. We are only helping them if we tell them what is true (See overview paragraphs 2–3).

   Bible references: 2 Corinthians 4:2; Matthew 5:18-19; 2 Peter 3:16.

   Questions: Who told Paul about Jesus? Did Paul make up things about God that sounded nicer, in case people didn't like truth?

2. The more we think about heaven the more we know how wonderful it will be – and we will want other people to be there with us (See overview paragraph 3).

   Bible references: 2 Corinthians 5:2-3, 8, 20; Psalm 119:19; Hebrews 11:16.

   Question: What made Paul keep going with his difficult job and want to tell people about Jesus?

3. God wants us to help others, for example with our time and money. The more we help, the more God will help us to help (See overview paragraph 5).

   Bible references: 2 Corinthians 1:3-4, 6; 9:10-11; Deuteronomy 15:11; Acts 2:44-45.

   Questions: Can you think of someone who is sad? Or people in the world that don't have enough money for food? How could you help those people?

SALVATION THREAD

Ambassadors are people sent to represent their own country in a foreign country. For example, America has an ambassador in London who represents America to Great Britain, and works for the benefit of America and Americans. Part of being a *Christian* is to be God's ambassador on earth. Christians belong to God and their real home is in *heaven*,[118] but they are here on earth to represent God to people.

Because of that, Christians must do what Paul the *apostle* did – tell other people the good news about God and live in a way that pleases God. Then no-one can look at us if we are Christians and say, "The Bible can't be true because this person likes to disobey God." This is what Paul meant when he wrote, "We put no stumbling block in anyone's path, so that our ministry will not be discredited."[119] Paul spent much of his letter explaining that he was living in obedience to God, and that the bad things people heard about Paul were just lies.

Key Verses: "Aim for perfection, listen to my appeal, be of one mind, live in peace. And the God of love and peace will be with you" (2 Corinthians 13:11).

"… thanks be to God, who always leads us in triumphal procession in Christ and through us spreads everywhere the fragrance of the knowledge of him" (2 Corinthians 2:14).

---

118. 2 Corinthians 5:1-9.
119. 2 Corinthians 6:3.

The book of
GALATIANS

GALATIANS

Don't try to change the gospel!

INTRODUCTION

- What would it feel like if someone followed you around, trying to undo everything you did? This is what Paul was going through when he wrote to the Galatians. When he and Barnabas left Galatia, other teachers went there saying wrong things about Jesus. Some people believed what those teachers said, so Paul wrote a letter to the churches to help them get back to the truth.

- Paul probably wrote this letter in about A.D. 48.

OVERVIEW

1. "This letter is from me, Paul the *apostle* (and my friends) – I was sent by God who saved me from my *sin*."

2. "I am very surprised that you are going away from God and his free gift of forgiveness. People tell you wrong things and God is very angry with them. I did not make up the good news about Jesus, and no-one forced me to tell you about it. I know about Jesus because Jesus himself told me."

3. "When I went to the church leaders in Jerusalem we agreed that I should take the good news about Jesus to lots of people who are not Jews. It was sad that Peter did not want to be with those people. He still didn't think they could be part of God's family and was afraid that some of his old friends would be cross with him if he liked them. I had to tell him he was very wrong."

4. "You foolish people … who tricked you about the good news of God's free gift? Did you think you were good enough to make God happy? Of course not! Not even the best people are good enough to do that. God came into your life because he loves you and you trusted him, not because you did good things."

5. "It is not true that if you do not follow God's laws perfectly he will not love you. God's rules are there to show you that you need Jesus and forgiveness."

6. "And you, Christians in Galatia, are God's children. You have Jesus in your heart. You have been set free from the wrong inside you. No one can say God doesn't love you just because you sometimes break his rules. Make sure you remember that."

7. "But that is not a reason to be deliberately sinful. We should use our freedom to please God by obeying him – that shows that we really love him."

LEARNING FROM GALATIANS

1. Sometimes we feel bad about doing the wrong thing. People might tell us we're not good enough for God, and then we try to do good things so that God will forgive us. That's what people were telling the Galatians, but it is not true because it is not what God says. He says that forgiveness is a free gift (See overview paragraphs 2, 4–6).

    Bible references: Galatians 1:6; 3:2; Zechariah 3:1-2; 1 John 1:9.

    Question: Can anyone be good enough to force God to let them into *heaven*?

2. God wants everyone to be with him – not just the nice people or the people from one country; not just boys or just girls, or just grown-ups or just children. Jesus died on the cross so that everyone who truly asks God will have their sins forgiven (See overview paragraph 3).

    Bible references: Galatians 2:9; Genesis 18:18; John 1:11-13.

    Question: If God wants everyone to believe in him, who should we tell about God's free gift of forgiveness?

3. If we really love God and he has forgiven our sins, more and more we will want to obey God. Ask him to help you with this (See overview paragraph 6).

    Bible references: Galatians 5:22-26; Psalm 119:10-11; John 14:15.

    Questions: When you are with your friends do you want to make them happy or sad? If we want to make our friends happy, how much more should we want to make God happy?

SALVATION THREAD

Paul warned the Galatians about people who said it wasn't enough to *repent* and believe in Jesus to have your sins forgiven. Those people changed the *gospel*, and said that people must also obey some Old Testament rules before they could be saved. This was dangerous teaching, because it meant people were trying to get to *heaven* by doing good things, rather than trusting God. Paul warned the Galatians about this.[120]

The truth of the *gospel* belongs to God. It comes from him,[121] and it never changes, so we must never try to change it. If we try to change it, even a little, then it is not the *gospel* any more. In fact, to say you only want to change the *gospel* a little is like saying you only want to poke one hole in a balloon – as soon as you've done that, it's not a balloon any more![122]

Key Verse: "Does God give you his Spirit and work miracles among you because you observe the *law*, or because you believe what you heard?" (Galatians 3:5).

---

120. Galatians 1:6-8.
121. Galatians 1:11-12.
122. Galatians 1:6-7.

The book of
EPHESIANS

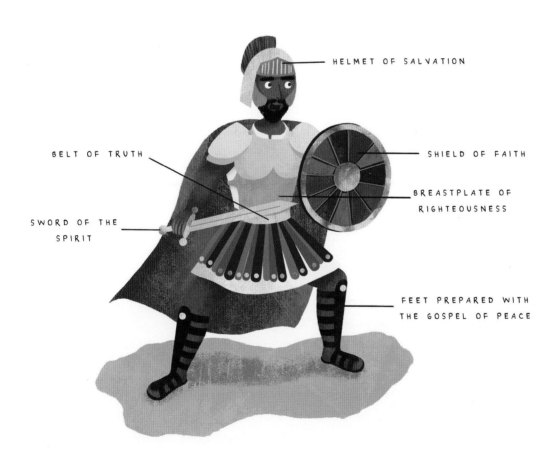

HELMET OF SALVATION

BELT OF TRUTH

SHIELD OF FAITH

BREASTPLATE OF RIGHTEOUSNESS

SWORD OF THE SPIRIT

FEET PREPARED WITH THE GOSPEL OF PEACE

EPHESIANS

Everything good is from God and by God

INTRODUCTION

- Have you ever paid someone for a Christmas present they gave you? Probably not! When Paul wrote to the Ephesians he tried to explain some things God said. One was that the free gift of forgiveness was just that … free! Ephesus was an important city in the country we now call Turkey. Paul stayed there for two or three years during one of his missionary journeys. He wrote this letter afterwards.

- Paul wrote this letter in A.D. 62.

OVERVIEW

1. "From Paul to the Christians in Ephesus. Praise God. He chose us - decided he would become our Father in *heaven*. Through Jesus' death on the *cross* and rising to life, God became our Father, and it brings him glory. When God saved you he gave you the Holy Spirit. Because he did that for you, I pray that you will know God better and understand how mighty he is, and how Jesus is in charge of everything."

2. "You used to be dead because of your *sin*. You were deliberately sinful and always did what you wanted, but you were made alive again, like Jesus was raised from the dead. We didn't do anything to save ourselves – God did it."

3. "I was sent to tell people from different countries about Jesus. God wants people all over the world to love him. I pray to God and I ask him to make you understand how much he loves you."

4. "Don't pretend to be better than anyone else, but love each other really well. Don't just do what you want to do. We should be more like God, who is full of love and loves us. Only say what is true, don't stay angry with people and don't be greedy or rude."

5. "You should not try and put yourselves ahead of each other. Mothers should not put themselves ahead of fathers. Fathers should love Mothers and do everything to help them, especially to help them love God. Jesus does this for all Christians. Children should obey their parents and not complain or argue. Fathers should not be mean to their children but teach them to know God."

6. "We all need to obey those in charge of us, even if they are not fair to us."

7. "Be strong in God and fight the *devil* like you're a soldier. Use God's armor: truth is your belt, being right with God is your chest-protector, trusting God is your shield,

God saving you is your helmet. With all these things you will be ready to serve God and pray for other Christians, including me."

LEARNING FROM EPHESIANS

1. If we are Christians it is because God chose us and saved us – not because of who we are or what we have done but because of his love. If you asked God to forgive your sins, thank him for his great love to you (See overview paragraphs 1–2, 4–5).

   Bible references: Ephesians 2:8-9; Deuteronomy 10:14; John 15:16.

   Questions: Who is the nicest person you know? Who is the most important person you can think of? Remember they need God just as much as you do.

2. God has instructions for every family member, to help us be more like God (See overview paragraphs 5–6).

   Bible references: Ephesians 5:22–6:4; Proverbs 22:6; Colossians 3:18-21.

   Question: What are God's rules in Ephesians for parents and children?

3. God gives us everything we need in order to love and obey him. Because God gives us all these things we can be safe with him forever (See overview paragraphs 1 and 7).

   Bible references: Ephesians 6:10-18; 1 Chronicles 29:14; John 14:23, 26.

   Questions: What has God given us? How can these things help us?

SALVATION THREAD

God chose the *Israelites* to be his special people. Through Jesus, the doors to God's kingdom have been opened to people all over the world. Non-Jews (Gentiles) as well as Jews are saved from *sin* if they believe in Jesus and *repent*. This was hard for some people to understand, and hard for some Jews to accept. Paul put it like this in Ephesians 3:6: "This mystery is that through the *gospel* the Gentiles are heirs together with Israel, members together of one body, and sharers together in the promise in Christ Jesus." In another letter Paul said, "There is neither Jew nor Greek, slave nor free, male nor female, for you are all one in Christ Jesus."[123]

Christians should realize, therefore, that what makes them like other Christians (their relationship with God), is more important than anything that makes them different (such as speaking a different language or having a different skin color).

Key Verse: "For it is by *grace* you have been saved, through *faith* – and this not from yourselves, it is the gift of God – not by works, so that no-one can boast. For we are God's workmanship, created in Christ Jesus to do good works, which God prepared in advance for us to do" (Ephesians 2:8-9).

---

123. Galatians 3:28.

The book of
PHILIPPIANS

PHILIPPIANS

Looking for encouragement to the perfect example: Jesus

INTRODUCTION

- Paul was back in prison (in Rome this time). When Paul was in Philippi, people started a riot because they were so angry with Paul's message about Jesus. He was put in jail, there was an earthquake, he got out of jail and was then asked to leave the city.[124] Later, he became a prisoner in Rome, so the Philippians gave Paul a gift. He wrote this letter to thank them, and encourage them to live like – and trust – Jesus. He also wanted the Philippians to know he was okay and the gospel was still being spread while he was in jail.

- Paul probably wrote this letter in A.D. 62.

OVERVIEW

1. "From Paul and Timothy to the Christians in Philippi. I thank God for you and your work for Jesus and I pray that you will become more like him all the time."

2. "Don't worry about me being in prison – more people are hearing about God because of it. I know I have a lot of work still to do for Jesus. I don't worry about dying – dying would be better for me because then I would be with Jesus in *heaven!*"

3. "Keep going even while people are being nasty to you because you are a *Christian*. Think about Jesus (who is God) and what he did for you in coming from *heaven* to earth to die on the *cross*. This should help you keep going – to want to do things for God and not be selfish. It should make you want to obey God in all things."

4. "I am going to send Timothy and Epaphroditus to you. They love God and you, so be kind to them."

5. "Watch out for those terrible people who tell you that you have to do enough good things before you are forgiven. I am thankful to God that he saved me because he is great, not because of anything I have done. When people are nasty to me because I love Jesus, I remind myself that I will one day go to be with Jesus forever."

6. "I must keep on going with God, and you must also. Be glad because of God. Trust him and don't worry. Obey his commands. I am happy that you have been very generous to me. Please keep it up as it is serving God."

7. "To God be the glory for ever and ever. Amen."

LEARNING FROM PHILIPPIANS

1. If God has forgiven our sins, then Jesus is our encouragement to serve God because we think of all he did for us. One day we will be with him in *heaven* for ever (See overview paragraphs 4 and 6).

---

124. Acts 16:12-40.

Bible references: Philippians 2:5-8; 1 Corinthians 2:2; Hebrews 12:2.

Questions: What are some of the wonderful things that Jesus did for people while he was on earth? What is the best thing he has done for you?

2. We must always trust God and love and obey him. That is sometimes very hard if we are worried, sad or in trouble. (See overview paragraphs 2–3 and 6).

Bible references: Philippians 1:27-28; 3:10-14; 4:6; Isaiah 12:2; Hebrews 10:36.

Questions: Why wasn't Paul worried about dying? Why was it a good thing that Paul was in prison?

3. It is God who saves us – not we who do enough good things to be forgiven. So we don't need to worry about whether we are good enough for God. We're not. That's why Jesus had to be perfect for us (See overview paragraphs 5–6).

Bible references: Philippians 3:1, 3, 8-9; Isaiah 64:6; Hebrews 10:14.

Question: Do you try to be good enough for God? Or do you trust him that he did everything that needs to be done?

SALVATION THREAD

Salvation threads run all through Scripture. A key one in Philippians points to Jesus as a suffering servant who dies to save his people and will reign forever as king of all creation.

"And being found in appearance as a man, he humbled himself and became obedient to death – even death on a cross! Therefore God exalted him to the highest place and gave him the name that is above every name, that at the name of Jesus every knee should bow, in *heaven* and on earth and under the earth ..." (Philippians 2:8-10).

Isaiah wrote about it 750 years earlier:

"[The Messiah] will have a heritage with the great, and he will have a part in the goods of war ... because he gave up his life...taking on himself the sins of the people, and making prayer for the wrongdoers" (Isaiah 53:12).

Jesus knew that prophecy was about him, and said, "I tell you that this scripture must be fulfilled in relation to me: And he was counted among criminals. Indeed, what's written about me is nearing completion" (Luke 22:37[125] – spoken in about A.D. 33).

One day Jesus will reign as king in heaven:

"Then I heard every creature in *heaven* and on earth and under the earth and on the sea, and all that is in them, singing: 'To him who sits on the throne and to the Lamb be praise and honor and *glory* and power, for ever and ever!' The four living creatures said, 'Amen', and the elders fell down and worshiped" (Revelation 5:13-14 – written in about A.D. 95).

Key Verse: "... God exalted him to the highest place and gave him the name that is above every name, that at the name of Jesus every knee should bow, in *heaven* and on earth and under the earth ..." (Philippians 2:9-10).

---

125. [Common English Bible translation].

The book of
COLOSSIANS

COLOSSIANS

Bringing it all back to Jesus

INTRODUCTION

- Most people feel sorry for themselves in prison, especially if they are innocent. Paul was in prison in Rome because people said he was a troublemaker, even though he spent his life trying to help people. While he was in prison he wrote letters to the Colossians, Ephesians and to Philemon. The Colossians were tricked into believing false teachings, so Paul had to remind them about what Jesus said, who he was, and what he had done.

- Paul probably wrote this letter in A.D. 62.

OVERVIEW

1. "From Paul and Timothy to the Christians in Colossae. *We always thank God … when we pray for you*[126] because of your *faith* in Jesus and love for other Christians, coming from your hope of *heaven* through the *gospel*. We have been praying that you will know more of God's will so that you can please him with how you live, giving thanks to God."

2. "Jesus made everything, was before everything, holds everything together, and is the leader of the church because he is fully God. God *reconciles* people to himself through the *sacrifice* of Jesus on the *cross*. No-one can accuse you of anything, if you keep trusting what God has done. This is the *gospel* being preached everywhere. I am a servant of that *gospel* that God sent to the Gentiles. I work hard and suffer because I want everyone to know Jesus so that they might be saved."

3. "Don't believe human ideas; keep trusting in Christ, who is fully God and fully man, in charge of everything. You were dead in your sins but God made you alive in Christ, forgiving your *sin* and defeating *Satan* on the *cross*. Don't worry if people criticize you for breaking their man-made religious rules, or if they boast about how spiritual they are."

4. "Jesus saved you from *sin* and death and you will be with him in *heaven*. So, get rid of all kinds of sin from your life like greed and lying. Instead, be kind, patient, forgiving and full of love. Fill yourself with Jesus' teachings, talk about them with each other, and do everything in the name of Jesus, giving thanks to God the Father. Do all your work as if it was directly for God."

---

126. Colossians 1:3.

5. "*Devote yourselves to prayer* ...[127] pray for us that we may have more opportunity to spread the *gospel*, and to do it clearly, even though I am in prison. Tychicus is coming to you with Onesimus, and he will give you my news. Other friends here say hello to you, including Mark and Luke."

6. "*Grace be with you.*"[128]

LEARNING FROM COLOSSIANS

1. Jesus is fully God and fully man. His words are perfect, and only through him can we be saved (See overview paragraphs 2–3).

   Bible references: Colossians 1:13-16; John 14:6; Hebrews 1:2-3.

   Question: What does this letter tell us about Jesus and what he's done?

2. The sins of Christians are forgiven by God because Jesus died and rose again. God did that work of forgiveness – it's finished. We don't need to, and can't, do anything to save ourselves (See overview paragraphs 2–3).

   Bible references: Colossians 1:22; Isaiah 45:17; John 19:30.

   Question: Do you think you could do enough good to be perfect? Nobody can! Thank God you don't have to be perfect, because Jesus has already been perfect for you.

3. Doing good things can't get us to *heaven*, but if we are saved from our sins and love God, then we will want to do good things and obey God (See overview paragraph 4).

   Bible references: Colossians 3:1; Leviticus 11:45; 1 John 2:5-6.

   Questions: If your sins are forgiven, do you thank God for doing that for you? What would you like to do for God?

SALVATION THREAD

After Jesus went to *heaven*, apostles like Paul went to different places and told people the *gospel* of Jesus Christ. Sadly, some other people told lies about the truth. For example, some said Jesus was not really God, or that you had to keep extra rules to go to *heaven*. Others told people to worship angels, or find out some important secret information.

Paul the *apostle* said none of that is true. He always pointed people back to Jesus, helped them to understand who Jesus was and what he did. When they understood Jesus they would understand the truth, be saved from their sins and grow closer to God.

The letter to Colossians is a big reminder that truth and life can only be found in Jesus.

Key Verse: "[God] ... has rescued us from the dominion of darkness and brought us into the kingdom of the Son he loves, in whom we have redemption, the forgiveness of sins" (Colossians 1:13-14).

---

127. Colossians 4:2.
128. Colossians 4:18.

The books of
1 & 2 THESSALONIANS

1 THESSALONIANS

Christ is coming again soon so live for him

INTRODUCTION

- Have people ever hated you so much that they started a riot? Probably not! But this is what happened to Paul. He was only in Thessalonica for a few weeks, and spoke at the synagogue. Lots of people put their trust in Jesus. Some Jews who didn't believe Jesus was God became jealous, because people no longer obeyed their man-made rules. So they started a riot to get Paul in trouble. Paul was then put in prison and had to escape from the city.[129] A few months later, Paul wrote this letter to the church in Thessalonica.

- Paul wrote this letter some time between A.D. 49 and 51.

OVERVIEW

1. "From me, Paul, and my friends Silas and Timothy. We thank God for your *faith* and love, and that God has chosen you to be with him. We thank him that you are carrying on being Christians even though people are being nasty to you about it."

2. "People were also nasty to us in Philippi before we came to see you. They didn't like that we believe in Jesus. Some people are now telling you that we only came to see you because we wanted money, or because we wanted to be in charge. That is not true – we only want to make God happy."

3. "We cared for you when we were with you and tried to help as much as we could, and did not ask you for any money. We thank God that you believe his good news, and still follow God when people are nasty about it. God will punish those people."

4. "I really miss you. I was afraid the *devil* might have tricked you about some things so I sent my good friend Timothy to help you, and to let me know how you are getting on. He has now returned and says that you are doing very well. This is great, and now I really want to come and see you."

5. "Make sure that you keep trying hard to please God: you must treat each other the right way, love each other more and not be lazy."

6. "Don't worry about what has happened to Christians who have died. Jesus will not forget them or miss them out when he comes again. If he comes again while you are still alive, they will see him even before you do! We don't know when Jesus will come again, so let's be ready for it by living for him."

---

129. Acts 17:1-10.

LEARNING FROM 1 THESSALONIANS

1. Many people don't believe that knowing Jesus is the only way for us to know God. Sometimes they get angry with us or even nasty. Ask God to help you love him and to love the people who are being nasty (See overview paragraphs 1–3).

    Bible references: 1 Thessalonians 2:2; Psalm 119:157; Matthew 5:44.

    Questions: How hard is it to be nice to people who are nasty to you? How do you feel when people are like that?

2. Paul was always kind to the Thessalonians. Paul wanted them to know that he told them about Jesus for their own good, not because he wanted something from them. We also should tell people about Jesus because we love Jesus and we love people (See overview paragraphs 2–4).

    Bible references: 1 Thessalonians 2:3, 5-6; Acts 4:20; 2 Corinthians 5:11-15.

    Questions: Paul couldn't be with the Thessalonians, so how did he help them? Paul focused on telling people about Jesus – how much do you think you should be telling people about Jesus?

3. Don't worry about when Jesus will come again – when he comes will be a surprise for everyone. Just get ready for Jesus by obeying him because you love him, and help other people to do the same thing (See overview paragraph 6).

    Bible references: 1 Thessalonians 5:1-2, 11; Psalm 37:7; Matthew 24:36-37.

    Questions: Why were the Thessalonians worried about Christians who had died? Why don't we need to worry about Christians who have died?

SALVATION THREAD

Jesus is coming back. We read about the first time he came in the gospels. We know that Jesus lived on earth for about thirty-three years before being killed and rising from the dead on the third day. After that he went back to be with God the Father in *heaven*.

The next time Jesus comes it will be Judgment Day. Everyone who rejected him will be put away from him forever, and his people will go to be with him forever. Even though God promised *salvation* to those who trust him and ask him for forgiveness, it's easy to get worried and to wonder whether it will really happen.

Some of the Thessalonians were worried about that, so Paul reminded them of an important truth: because God chose to save us, and because forgiveness is a gift from him (we didn't earn it) we are therefore safe in him. Paul said the Thessalonians should encourage each other with this truth.[130]

Key Verse: "For God chose to save us through our Lord Jesus Christ, not to pour out his anger on us. Christ died for us so that, whether we are dead or alive when he returns, we can live with him forever" (1 Thessalonians 5:9-10, NLT).

---

130. 1 Thessalonians 5:9-11.

2 THESSALONIANS

Keep on keeping on and waiting for Christ

INTRODUCTION

- Sometimes a sports team who are winning, think they hear the final whistle and stop playing, only to find the whistle came from someone in the crowd and not the referee. The Thessalonians were like that – they thought Jesus' second coming was happening so soon that they could literally sit down and wait for it to happen. That's what they hoped, because they really wanted Jesus to come again. Paul encouraged them to keep working for Jesus, even when life was hard.

- Paul wrote this letter between A.D. 49 and 51, shortly after 1 Thessalonians.

OVERVIEW

1. "From me, Paul, and my friends Silas and Timothy."

2. "It is great that your *faith* and love keep growing, even though life is very hard for you, and people are nasty to you because you believe in Jesus. We tell people about how well you are doing. God always does the best thing and he is always fair. This means that when Jesus comes again you will have no more trouble. But there will be trouble for people who are nasty to you, and those who say no to God."

3. "We pray that you will keep trying to do what God wants, and that he will help you do all the good things you want to do. This will help you and other people to love Jesus."

4. "Some of you think Jesus already came back to earth again. He hasn't. Other things have to happen first, including God defeating an enemy who wants to take people away from God."

5. "I'm so glad God chose to save you, through the good news we told you about Jesus. Make sure you continue to believe that good news, and do good things for God."

6. "Please pray for us that the good news about Jesus would go to lots of places, and that people will believe it and love Jesus, just like you do. Pray that we will be protected from people who want to hurt us. We know God will protect you and help you love him."

7. "It is important to keep away from people who call themselves Christians, but who refuse to do any work. God made us to work, and we should always try to do what God says."

8. "Everything we are telling you here is really important. I pray that God will give you peace."

LEARNING FROM 2 THESSALONIANS

1. God helps us to keep going by reminding us that he always does the right thing. If God has forgiven our sins, one day we will be with him in *heaven* forever. Everyone who says no to the free gift of forgiveness will be punished forever (See overview paragraph 2).

   Bible references: 2 Thessalonians 1:5-6, 8-9; Matthew 25:46; Psalm 7:9, 17.
   Question: Are you afraid that if you tell people about Jesus, they might be mean to you or laugh at you?

2. Jesus will come again, but it has not happened yet. We don't need to think about when it's going to happen – just believe in God and do good things for him. (See overview paragraphs 3–5).

   Bible references: 2 Thessalonians 2:1-3, 15; 1 Thessalonians 5:1-2; Matthew 25:13.
   Questions: Do you look forward to when Jesus comes again? Why?

3. It is important that more and more people know and love Jesus. He came to save us from our sins. Ask God to help you tell people about him. (See overview paragraph 6).

   Bible references: 2 Thessalonians 3:1-5; Acts 20:24; 1 Corinthians 2:2.
   Questions: How important do you think Paul thought it was to tell people about Jesus? Why?

SALVATION THREAD

Some people are waiting for Jesus and they think they're okay with God. They want heaven, but they're not interested in serving God or telling people about Jesus.

Paul reminded the Thessalonians, and his letter reminds us, that waiting for Jesus to come again means perseverance. We need to work hard for God and keep on trusting him for forgiveness, even when we're tired, and even if we're suffering. When we persevere, we can have confidence that God "called you to this through [the] *gospel*, that you might share in the *glory* of our Lord Jesus Christ,"[131] and that "the Lord is faithful, and he will strengthen and protect you from the evil one."[132]

Key Verse: "May our Lord Jesus Christ himself and God our Father, who loved us and by his *grace* gave us eternal encouragement and good hope, encourage your hearts and strengthen you in every good deed and word" (2 Thessalonians 2:16-17).

---

131. 2 Thessalonians 2:14.
132. 2 Thessalonians 3:3.

The books of
1 & 2 TIMOTHY

1 TIMOTHY

Protecting God's church

INTRODUCTION

- While Paul went to Macedonia to spread the gospel, he sent Timothy to Ephesus to help the church get organized, and to ensure the right things were being taught. Paul wanted to join Timothy there, but then he realized he might be delayed, so contacted Timothy with advice and instruction. Timothy was one of Paul's closest and most trusted friends. He was named with Paul as the sender of six of Paul's letters.

- Paul wrote this letter some time between A.D. 64 and 66.

OVERVIEW

1. "From Paul, an *apostle* of Jesus, *To Timothy my true son in the faith* ...[133] Please stay in Ephesus to command men not to spread false teaching or concentrate on things that don't matter. They should stop wanting so badly to be teachers, and instead focus on loving people."

2. "*Christ Jesus came into the world to save sinners,*[134] and because of the *grace* he showed me despite all my *sin*, people can see how patient God is. Hold on to the *faith*. Some people haven't done that, and they've made a mess of their lives. Men should be full of prayer, with no anger or arguing. Women should be humble and submissive. Elders and deacons must be people who behave in a godly way, and elders must be able to teach."

3. "Some people will abandon the *faith* and follow false teachings, including extra rules that don't come from God. Follow God's rules. Help people spot and avoid false teachings. We *have put our hope in the living God,*[135] not in anything we do. Teach these things, live a godly life, and *devote yourself to the public reading of Scripture, to preaching and to teaching.*[136] Keep going with this, *because if you do, you will save both yourself and your hearers.*"[137]

4. "Treat older people with great respect and younger people like your brothers and sisters. Make sure that people look after their own families instead of expecting everyone else to do it."

5. "If anyone deliberately teaches wrong things about the Bible and about Jesus, that means they think too much of themselves and understand nothing. They are troublemakers who try to get rich through people giving them money. We shouldn't focus on getting

---

133. 1 Timothy 1:2.
134. 1 Timothy 1:15.
135. 1 Timothy 4:10.
136. 1 Timothy 4:13.
137. 1 Timothy 4:16.

more money, but be content with what we have. If we love money it leads to all kinds of evil and can lead people away from Jesus. Run away from those things, and run towards having more *faith*, love and gentleness, and defending the truth about God."

6. "Grace be with you all."[138]

LEARNING FROM 1 TIMOTHY

1. Don't let anyone tell you that you need to understand some complicated ideas or do enough good things before God will accept you. Forgiveness is a free gift from God. When people make up extra rules they don't help people towards God, they take people away from him (See overview paragraphs 1– 3).

   Bible references: 1 Timothy 1:8-9, 14; Matthew 15:9; 23:13-15.

   Question: To be given God's "grace" (v. 14) means to get something for free from God that you don't deserve. God's forgiveness comes from his *grace*, so what do you think God is like?

2. God wants his people – his church – to support and defend the truth about him, so God told Timothy through Paul what a good church looks like. That included good leadership (elders and deacons), lots of praying for people and a focus on God rather than us (See overview paragraphs 1–5).

   Bible references: 1 Timothy 3:14-15 (all of chapters 2–3); Psalm 25:4-5; Jude 3.

   Questions: What could you pray for churches, or for the church you go to?

3. If we are Christians it changes the way we live. We won't want to live sinful lives any more; instead, we want to obey God (See overview paragraphs 2 and 5).

   Bible references: 1 Timothy 6:11-12; Psalm 119:66; Ephesians 4:22-24.

   Questions: Read 1 Timothy 6:11. What do you think it means to "pursue" those ways of living and behaving? How can you do that?

SALVATION THREAD

There is a right and there is a wrong. There is a message that IS the gospel, and there are many messages that are NOT the *gospel*. Paul made that clear to Timothy when he wrote things like, "... God our Savior, who wants all men to be saved and to come to a knowledge of the truth" (2:4), mentioned "truths of the faith" (4:6) and told Timothy to "guard what has been entrusted to your care. Turn away from ... what is falsely called knowledge" (6:20).

Many people in the time of Paul and Timothy thought there was either no truth, or several versions of the truth, or that it didn't really matter what you believed. When Paul wrote this letter he wanted Timothy to understand he had been given the truth, and it needed to be guarded. That's one reason why God included real letters in the Bible. It's not a textbook about being a *Christian*, it shows us what God has been doing with people and how he has protected the truth about himself. Praise him that he keeps doing those things today!

Key Verse: "Although I hope to come to you soon, I am writing you these instructions so that, if I am delayed, you will know how people ought to conduct themselves in ... the church of the living God, the pillar and foundation of the truth" (1 Timothy 3:14-15).

---

138. 1 Timothy 6:21 [NIV 2011.

2 TIMOTHY

Famous last words

INTRODUCTION

- Paul knew when he wrote this that he didn't have long to live. He was in prison in Rome, and would never get out. But he would soon be free – free with God in heaven. He looked forward to that, while he encouraged Timothy to persevere. Timothy was much younger than Paul and had lots of work still to do.. Helping others to know God better was what mattered most to Paul. So this – his last letter – was all about that.

- Paul wrote this letter some time between A.D. 64 and 67, after 1 Timothy.

OVERVIEW

1. "From Paul, an apostle of Jesus by God's will, *to Timothy, my dear son.*[139] I thank God for you in my prayers and long to see you. ... *fan into flame the gift of God*[140] and serve him in a spirit of power, love and self-discipline."

2. "Jesus, *destroyed death and ... brought life and immortality to light through the gospel,*[141] and I am suffering because people are trying to stop me share the *gospel.* Join me in that suffering, and don't be ashamed of the gospel or me. Hold on to the truth about Jesus that I passed on to you."

3. "Find reliable men and have them teach people about Jesus. Do your best to honor God in everything you do and handle God's word of truth correctly. *Everyone who confesses the name of the Lord must turn away from wickedness,*[142] *... and pursue righteousness, faith, love and peace ... Don't have anything to do with foolish and stupid arguments ...*"[143]

4. "There will be terrible times. *People will be lovers of themselves, lovers of money, boastful ... disobedient to their parents ... [and] ... without love.*[144] These people claim to know God, but they don't live like it and they oppose the truth; stay away from them. All Scripture is breathed out by God, and is good for preparing you for all you should do."

5. "Preach the Bible; encourage people, put them right when they go against the Bible. Do this carefully and gently in the hope that God will take them to repentance and knowledge of the truth. Some day people won't put up with right teaching, and will just listen to what they like. Beware of Alexander the metalworker, because he strongly opposes the *gospel.*"

---

139. 2 Timothy 1:2.
140. 2 Timothy 1:6.
141. 2 Timothy 1:10.
142. 2 Timothy 2:19.
143. 2 Timothy 2:22-23.
144. 2 Timothy 3:2-3.

6. "During my first trial, everyone left me; *But the Lord stood at my side and gave me strength, so that through me the message might go to Gentiles everywhere.*[145] I am nearly finished with my life's work, and *The Lord … will bring me safely to his heavenly kingdom. To him be the glory for ever and ever. Amen.*"[146]

LEARNING FROM 2 TIMOTHY

1. God wants Christians to persevere in what they believe and in telling other people about the *gospel*, even though people may treat them badly because of it. Paul was in prison and would soon be killed, because he told people the truth about Jesus. If Paul could persevere in God's strength, then so can we! (See overview paragraphs 1–2, 5–6).

   Bible references: 2 Timothy 3:12-14; Acts 5:40-42; Romans 8:37-39.

   Question: If you believe in God and the Bible, how does it make you feel that some of the people around you don't believe?

2. God tells Christians that they must obey him – not because it will save them from their sins, but because God has already saved them from their sins. Everyone who is truly saved from *sin* doesn't want to *sin* any more (See overview paragraphs 3–4).

   Bible references: 2 Timothy 2:19, 22; John 15:10; Romans 6:10–11.

   Question: What would you say to someone who claimed they loved their parents, but didn't want to obey them?

3. The truth about God is in the Bible. We can know if people are telling us the truth by checking it with what God says in the Bible. Paul reminded Timothy how important it is to teach people from the Bible, even when people don't like to hear about it (See overview paragraphs 3–5).

   Bible references: 2 Timothy 3:15-16; Deuteronomy 5:27; John 17:17.

   Question: If you want to know what someone thinks about something, who should you ask? In the same way, if you want to know what God thinks about something, where should you go to find out?

SALVATION THREAD

In this letter Paul was urging Timothy to persevere, warning against false teaching, and encouraging him to stay faithful to the truth. Paul was saying "Nothing is more important than the truth of the *gospel!*" The whole of the Old Testament pointed to it, and Jesus fulfilled it. Then the apostles spread it, wrote about it, and in many cases, died for it. The gospel of Jesus Christ meant everything to Paul, and it should mean light, eternity, and everything to us.

Key Verse: "All Scripture is God-breathed and is useful for teaching, rebuking, correcting and training in righteousness, so that the man of God may be thoroughly equipped for every good work" (2 Timothy 3:16-17).

---

145. 2 Timothy 4:17.
146. 2 Timothy 4:18.

The book of
TITUS

TITUS

Straighten out the church[147]

INTRODUCTION

- There was a lot of work unfinished when Paul left Crete. During an earlier part of this missionary journey Titus had become a *Christian*. Now, with Titus a trusted friend back in Crete, Paul wrote to help him organize the churches on the island. Paul wanted to make sure the right things were taught. It was a big job for Titus, but Paul respected him greatly, and wanted Titus to go back to Paul as soon as the job was done.[148]

- Paul wrote this letter some time between A.D. 64 and 66.

OVERVIEW

1. "Paul, a servant and *apostle* of God for the *faith* of those God has chosen, and for knowledge of the truth that leads to having a right relationship with God. A truth that sits on God's promise of eternal life."

2. "I left you in Crete to finish sorting things out with the churches, like putting elders in charge. Elders must be men who love God and who show this by the way they live. They must understand God's free gift of forgiveness, and not let anyone ruin lives by teaching that God's gift is not free, or by teaching other wrong things about God."

3. "Teach the Bible to everyone, and make sure you teach what it really says. Set such a good example that no-one will have a good reason to say bad things about how you behave. God's *grace* has saved us from our sins and God's *grace* teaches us to live good lives for God, while we wait for Jesus to come again."

4. "Remind the people to obey those who are in charge, and to look for chances to do good things. Our old sinful nature made us want to do bad things, but then Jesus saved us and gave us the Holy Spirit. Now we can look forward to being in *heaven* forever."

5. "Don't have silly arguments and don't put up with someone who wants people in the church to start going against each other."

6. "People must understand how important it is to obey God and do what is right."

7. "Please come and spend some time with me in Nicopolis, and say hello to all the Christians in Crete from me."

---

147. See Titus 1:5. 'Straighten out', 'put in order' and 'complete the work' are some of the translations of what Paul told Titus to do to the church in Crete.
148. See Titus 3:12.

226

LEARNING FROM TITUS

1. It is important to understand the Bible, especially God's free gift of forgiveness (See overview paragraphs 2–4).

   Bible references: Titus 3:4-7; Nehemiah 8:3; Matthew 22:29.

   Question: What happens to people's lives if they don't understand that God's gift of forgiveness is free?

2. We all need reminding to obey God, because we all easily become disobedient. It is kind for someone to remind us, because disobedience to God spoils our relationship with him (See overview paragraphs 3–4 and 6).

   Bible references: Titus 2:11-14; Jeremiah 14:10; Romans 7:14-15.

   Question: In what ways are you tempted to disobey God? Ask God to help you with those things.

3. God wants churches to be healthy. Three important things for that are: good leaders, good teaching and people in the churches who are together, not going against each other (See overview paragraphs 2 and 5).

   Bible references: Titus 1:5, 9; 3:10; Exodus 18:21; 2 Timothy 2:2.

   Questions: If you go to church, do you pray for it to have good leaders and teachers? And do you pray for your parents to be good parents for you?

SALVATION THREAD

When Jesus died and rose again, he didn't do it to get people free tickets to *heaven* while they carried on behaving as they did before. Jesus' work in *salvation* was to make everything good again that once was bad. That means that if we have our sins forgiven, then Jesus' work in our lives has just started.

Paul told Titus that Jesus "gave himself for us to redeem us from all wickedness and to purify for himself a people that are his very own, eager to do what is good."[149] "I want you to stress these things," Paul wrote later, "so that those who have trusted God may be careful to devote themselves to doing what is good."[150] After we have been saved from sin, God wants his people to become more and more like him – wanting to do what is right, not wanting to do what is wrong.[151]

Key Verse: "But when the kindness and love of God our Savior appeared, he saved us, not because of righteous things we had done, but because of his *mercy*" (Titus 3:4-5).

---

149. Titus 2:14.
150. Titus 3:8.
151. Titus 2:11-12.

The book of

PHILEMON

PHILEMON

A slave becomes a brother

INTRODUCTION

- Onesimus used to be Philemon's slave, but he ran away (probably after stealing from Philemon). While he was away he became a *Christian* after hearing the *gospel* from the *apostle* Paul. Paul wrote this letter to Philemon, asking him to receive Onesimus back as a brother (a fellow *Christian*), and not to have him or treat him as a slave any more.

- Paul probably wrote this letter around A.D. 62.

OVERVIEW

1. From *"Paul, a prisoner of Christ Jesus, and Timothy our brother, To Philemon our dear friend and fellow worker, to Apphia our sister, to Archippus our fellow soldier and to the church that meets in your home: Grace to you and peace from God our Father and the Lord Jesus Christ."*[152]

2. "I always thank my God as I remember you in my prayers, because I hear about your faith in the Lord Jesus and your love for all the saints,[153] which encourages me."

3. *"I pray that you may be active in sharing your faith, so that you will have a full understanding of every good thing we have in Christ.*[154] Because of your love, I will ask you, even though I could tell you what to do about Onesimus, who became a *Christian.*"

4. "He was useless to you before, but now he is useful and dear to both of us. I wanted to keep him with me to help me while I am in prison here, but I'm sending him back to you. He will return to you not as a slave, but as a brother in Christ."

5. "So please, welcome him as you would welcome me. If he owes you anything, I will repay it (even though you owe me everything because I shared the gospel with you). This will encourage me, and I know you will do even more than I ask."

6. "Finally, please get a guest room ready for me as I hope to come back to you soon. My fellow prisoner Epaphras says hello, and so do other fellow workers for Jesus."

7. "The grace of the Lord Jesus Christ be with your spirit."[155]

---

152. Philemon verses 1-3.
153. Philemon verse 4.
154. Philemon verse 6.
155. Philemon verse 25.

LEARNING FROM PHILEMON

1. It is good to pray to God for other people. Paul thanked God because he could see what God was doing to make Philemon more holy and more loving towards other Christians (See overview paragraphs 2–3).

    Bible references: Philemon 4-7; 1 Samuel 12:23; 1 Corinthians 1:4-5.

    Questions: Who can you thank God for?

2. How can Christians show love to each other? We don't love people just because they are nice to us. We love other Christians because God loves them and because God loves us (See overview paragraphs 2–3).

    Bible references: Philemon 5, 7, 9; Leviticus 19:18; John 13:35.

    Questions: Why is love such an important part of being a *Christian*? Can you think how Christians can show love to each other?

3. When God forgives us our sins, we are not just a little forgiven. No, when he saves us we are made totally right with God. He treats us not as slaves but as his friends. This means we are *reconciled* to God, by God. Onesimus couldn't *reconcile* himself with Philemon, because he was the one who had gone away. We can't *reconcile* ourselves with God, because we are the ones who have gone away from God. But God does it for us – what an amazing gift! (See overview paragraphs 4–5).

    Bible references: Philemon 16; Jeremiah 33:8; Colossians 1:22.

    Questions: What does it feel like when you have an argument with someone you love? What does it feel like when you make up (are *reconciled*)? Imagine that – times a thousand – and you will begin to understand what it is like to be *reconciled* with God.

SALVATION THREAD

We are all born as slaves to *sin* – that means, we do what *sin* says in our hearts and we don't want to worship or serve God. If we accept God's free gift of forgiveness, asking him to take away our sins and trusting in Jesus, we are no longer slaves to *sin*.

Onesimus didn't deserve to have Philemon take him back. We don't deserve to have God take us back. But we can thank God that he loves to free us from the slavery of *sin*. He loves to treat us as his children even though we owe him everything and don't deserve his love. Paul says that Philemon owed Paul everything just because Paul told him about the *gospel*! That's how precious the *gospel* is!

Key Verse: "Your love has given me great joy and encouragement, because you, brother, have refreshed the hearts of the saints" (Philemon 7).

The book of

HEBREWS

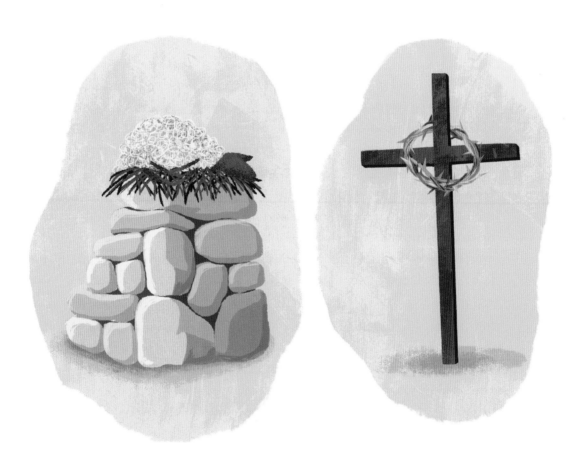

HEBREWS

It's all about Jesus

INTRODUCTION

- Discouraged? Tempted to give up and go back to an easier life? Not learning anything? Many Jewish Christians felt that way in the decades after Jesus went back to heaven. This letter pointed them to Jesus to encourage them. The author was probably Luke, Paul or Apollos, but we don't know. It was written to Jewish people (also called 'Hebrews') who were Christians. It talks a lot about what happened with priests and sacrifices and how it all pointed to Jesus. It's a great book to help us understand how the Old Testament fits with the New Testament.

- Hebrews was probably written some time between A.D. 30 and 70.

OVERVIEW

1. *"In the past God spoke to our forefathers through the prophets at many times and in various ways, but in these last days he has spoken to us by his Son,*[156] who made the universe with God and rules over everything. Jesus is superior to the angels, to Moses, and to all the high priests. So listen, believe and have faith in him."

2. "Don't ignore what God says but encourage people to hold on to the truth about Jesus. Remember, the *Israelites* who didn't believe in God were not allowed into the *promised land*. Don't be like that and miss out on being with God forever! Hearing the truth is not enough – you need to believe it and have *faith*. Jesus understands everything you're going through because he has gone through it himself, and he loves to help us when we pray to him."

3. "God prophesied through Jeremiah that he would make a new *covenant* to replace the old one. He said about his people, '*I will forgive their wickedness and remember their sins no more.*'[157] '*The law is only a shadow of the good things that are coming – not the realities themselves.*'[158] Animal sacrifices did not save anyone, but they reminded people of their sin. With the new *covenant*, the once and for all *sacrifice* of Jesus is what saves people. Because we know this let's go to God, trusting him, knowing that he can take our sins away. Let's think about how we can encourage each other to do good things and be full of love."

4. *"... Faith is being sure of what we hope for and certain of what we do not see,*[159] and it is by *faith* we know God. All the great people in the Old Testament had *faith* – people like Noah, Abraham, Joseph and Moses. They are watching us from *heaven*,

---

156. Hebrews 1:1-2.
157. Hebrews 8:12.
158. Hebrews 10:1.
159. Hebrews 11:1.

so let's get rid of the *sin* and everything else that pushes us away from God. Make sure you stick to the truth about God, and don't say no to Jesus or his warnings about *sin*."

LEARNING FROM HEBREWS

1. Listening to and believing in Jesus is most important because Jesus is most important. He made and rules everything, and he is greater than everything and everyone that was made. And yet he came to earth as a *sacrifice* so that sins can be forgiven (See overview paragraphs 1–2 and 4).

   Bible references: Hebrews 1:1-4; 2:1-3; Psalm 110:1-2; Matthew 3:17.

   Questions: Who is the most important person you have met? Why do you think Jesus is more important than him or her?

2. Sometimes we are tempted to turn away from what God said, because it's hard or we see other people aren't doing it. We must persevere in trusting and obeying Jesus (See overview paragraphs 1–2 and 4).

   Bible references: Hebrews 10:23, 35-36; 1 Kings 18:21-22; Matthew 13:20-22.

   Questions: Do any of your friends or other people at school believe in God? If not, what do they say about it? How does that make you feel?

3. Everything that needed to happen for people to be saved from their sins has been done. Jesus is the *sacrifice* that means no more sacrifices need to be made – the penalty for *sin* was paid forever (See overview paragraph 3).

   Bible references: Hebrews 10:14, 17-18; Jeremiah 33:14-16; Romans 8:31.

   Questions: Do you accept that Jesus is God? Do you trust God that through Jesus' death and resurrection all your sins are forgiven? (Hebrews 10:10).

SALVATION THREAD

"Here I am – it is written about me in the scroll – I have come to do your will, O God" (Hebrews 10:7).

"And beginning with Moses and all the Prophets, [Jesus] explained to them what was said in all the Scriptures concerning himself" (Luke 24:27).

The whole Bible points to Jesus. The sacrifices in the Old Testament pointed to how serious *sin* is, and to how one day the ultimate *sacrifice* would pay the penalty for the sins of God's people. That's why God's people in the Old Testament understood that the sacrifices themselves weren't the important thing – what was important then and now is *faith* in God (Hebrews 11:1-2).

The writer wanted people to understand that Jesus is greater than all, and showed it by comparing him to the angels, priests and Moses. Moses was one of the greatest Jews ever, and respected. But the writer pointed out that although Moses was a good servant and leader, Jesus was and is a perfect servant, faithful leader, and the one who brings forgiveness for his people's sins (Hebrews 3:5-6).

Key Verse: "May the God of peace, who through the blood of the eternal *covenant* brought back from the dead our Lord Jesus, that great Shepherd of the sheep, equip you with everything good for doing his will, and may he work in us what is pleasing to him, through Jesus Christ, to whom be *glory* for ever and ever. Amen" (Hebrews 13:20-21).

The book of
JAMES

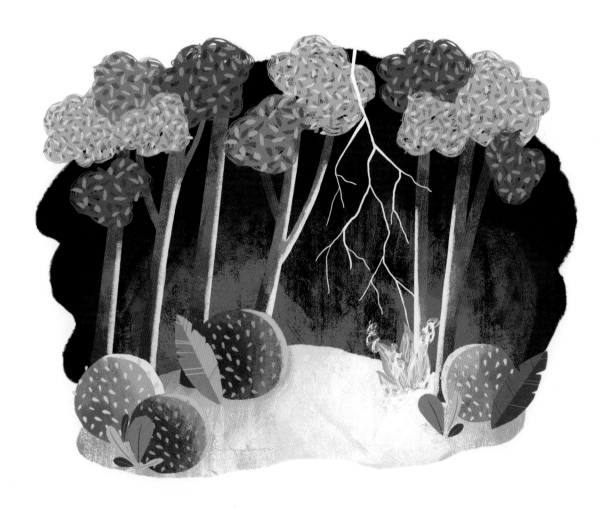

JAMES

Saved by faith alone, but not by faith that is alone[160]

INTRODUCTION

- James was Jesus' brother and the leader of the church in Jerusalem in the time of the apostles. This may have been the first book of the New Testament to be written, probably only about ten years after Jesus went back to heaven. James wanted Christians to keep going, and to live in a way that pleased God.

- James wrote his letter probably some time between A.D. 42 and 47.

OVERVIEW

1. "From James, a servant of God the Father and Jesus, to Jewish Christians all over the world."

2. "*Consider it pure joy, my brothers, whenever you face [difficulties] of many kinds,*[161] because they help you develop perseverance, which helps you to know God better. Those who persevere will receive a crown of life from God."

3. "*Sin* comes when we are dragged away from God in our heads by wanting to do wrong things, so stay away from anything that makes you want to *sin. Do not merely listen to the word, and so deceive yourselves – do what it says. Otherwise you're like someone who sees their own face in a mirror, and then goes away and forgets what they look like… Faith by itself, if it is without action, is dead.*[162] Just believing that there is one God, and not doing anything about it, doesn't do any good. Even devils believe there is only one God."

4. "Ships are steered by a small rudder. In the same way, *the tongue is a small part of the body, but it makes great boasts. Think 'what a great forest is set on fire by a small spark'*[163] – a person can ruin their life through the things they say. If we love God we should only be saying good things."

5. "You keep arguing and fighting because you want things that you don't have, and when you ask God for things it is for bad reasons like being selfish. When you make plans, remember that it all depends on God whether you can carry out those plans, so there's no point boasting. Sinning is not just doing bad things; it's not doing the good things you should do."

6. "Be patient and stand firm as you wait for Jesus to come again. Don't grumble or say bad things about each other. Follow the example of people like Job[164] who persevered

---

160. Those words were written by Martin Luther, a famous Christian from 500 years ago who translated the Bible into German. His teachings helped many people to understand that they didn't have to pay money or do enough good things to get to heaven. Instead, he showed people from the Bible that they must trust in Jesus to save them through his death and resurrection.
161. James 1:2.
162. James 1:22 and 2:17.
163. James 3:5.
164. See the book of Job in the Bible.

through suffering. Pray in *faith*, and help people come back to the truth about God if they wander away from it."

LEARNING FROM JAMES

1. James reminds us that being a *Christian* is not easy. We should remember that bad times are opportunities to get to know God better. We must rely on God to keep us going. Even in bad times, God is being good to his people and we can thank him for that (See overview paragraphs 2 and 6).

   Bible references: James 1:2-4, 12; 5:8; Psalm 27:14; 1 Peter 4:12-13.

   Questions: How is it hard to be a *Christian?* Can you think of anyone in the Bible who suffered because they obeyed God or believed in Jesus?

2. Just knowing the truth isn't any good; we need to do something about it. A *Christian* knows that they are a sinner needing God's forgiveness and they *repent*. Then their behavior and how they talk begins to show that they repented. If we are sorry for our sin we don't want to sin any more (See overview paragraph 3).

   Bible references: James 1:22-25; 2:26; Hosea 8:2; Matthew 7:21.

   Questions: If you looked in the mirror and saw dirt on your face, what would you do? When we look into God's *law* we find that we cannot keep it – what should we do about that?

3. What we say is important. We can use our words to praise God, thank him, and tell people about him … but we can also lie and say unkind or disobedient words (See overview paragraph 4).

   Bible references: James 3:8-9; Proverbs 12:6; 1 Peter 3:10.

   Questions: How easy is it to control what you say so that you only say good things? When do you find it hard?

SALVATION THREAD

"… it is by *grace* you have been saved, through *faith* – and this not from yourselves, it is the gift of God – not by works, so that no-one can boast" (Ephesians 2:8-9, written by Paul the *apostle*).

"You see that a person is *justified* by what he does and not by *faith* alone … As the body without the spirit is dead, so *faith* without deeds is dead" (James 2:24, 26).

James' letter can be confusing, because he writes so much about what we must DO. Paul wrote more about how we can't DO anything to be saved by God. Did James and Paul disagree with each other? No, Paul and James totally agreed, which is not surprising when you remember that the Bible is God's Word. They did not make things up, they received knowledge from God.

Paul was writing to people who were doing good things so that God would like them. He had to tell them that was impossible, and that they needed to trust God instead. The people James was writing to had the opposite problem: they thought that as long as you believed that God exists, you would be saved. James had to remind them that even the devils believe that, and if we have truly repented, we will try to obey God.

Key Verse: "Resist the Devil and he will flee from you. Come near to God and he will come near to you" (James 4:7-8).

The books of
1 & 2 PETER

1 PETER

Strength for the suffering Christians

INTRODUCTION

- Peter was probably in Rome when he wrote this. Paul had been let out of prison and went to a different country for a while. Mark was with Peter, and Silas probably helped Peter to write the letter. Peter wrote to Christians everywhere, encouraging them to keep loving God and other people, even when life was very hard.

- Peter probably wrote this letter in A.D. 62/63.

OVERVIEW

1. "From Peter, an *apostle* of Jesus Christ. To God's chosen people, scattered to many different places."

2. "Praise God that he saved us and keeps us with him until we get to *heaven*. You are going through some difficult times but God uses them to show that your *faith* is real, that you are not just pretending to love God. Don't be surprised when things are difficult or people are nasty."

3. "Because God is giving you his free gift of forgiveness, and because God is *holy*, we should try to be *holy*, which means obeying God. Remember that God has saved you forever and that it cannot be undone. Jesus is really special to you and he chose you to serve him."

4. "We should obey people if they are in charge of us, even if they are not nice. If we believe in Jesus but like to be sinful, other people might think that Jesus doesn't care about *sin* and bad behavior. Then they won't want to be sorry to him. Be kind to everyone, whether they are nice to you or not."

5. "Your mother is just as special as your father. She should let your father be in charge of the family. When mothers do this well it makes them beautiful – not just beautiful to look at, but beautiful in their minds and thoughts. Fathers should take special care of mothers and not be bossy."

6. "We should be like Jesus, and not just think about what we want, but how to obey God and love others. Put other people ahead of yourself and trust God about everything. You can do this because he cares about you, which also means that you should tell him about whatever makes you worried."

7. "Keep hold of these true things about God that I have told you. They are meant to help you keep going and not give up."

LEARNING FROM 1 PETER

1. If we are sad or people are being nasty to us, it does not mean God has forgotten us. If we have asked God to forgive our sins and we trust God, Satan cannot take us away from God (See overview paragraphs 2 and 3).

   Bible references: 1 Peter 1:3-7; Deuteronomy 31:8; Romans 8:39.

   Questions: What good things can you tell yourself about God, when people are being nasty to you?

2. If your teacher or a parent is not being nice, you might think it is okay to disobey them. But God says whether they are nice or not nice, we need to do as they say (See overview paragraph 4).

   Bible references: 1 Peter 2:13; Exodus 20:12; Matthew 22:21.

   Questions: When do you find it easy to do as you are told? When do you find it difficult? Ask God to help you with the difficult times.

3. Obeying God isn't like having a rule book that we don't care about. If we asked God for his free gift of forgiveness then we have the greatest gift ever, and now we want to obey God because we love him, just like Jesus showed us to do (See overview paragraphs 3 and 6).

   Bible references: 1 Peter 1:23–2:3; Exodus 20:1; John 15:9-10.

   Question: What reasons did Peter give for obeying God?

SALVATION THREAD

The strength to keep going and have joy, even when times are hard, comes partly from knowing where you are going. Christians know that God is looking after them, and that he is getting a place ready for them in heaven.[165] If our sins are forgiven, we belong to God and Jesus has defeated death ... so why is everything still so hard?

Peter reminds us to expect hard times in life, and to remember that God's promise to us, if we repent, is not that life will be easy or comfortable. God's promise is that we will be with him and he will be with us forever because we have "received mercy"[166] from God and belong with him.

Key Verse: "And the God of all *grace*, who called you to his eternal *glory* in Christ, after you have suffered a little while, will himself restore you and make you strong, firm and steadfast" (1 Peter 5:10).

---

165. 1 Peter 1:3-6.
166. 1 Peter 2:10.

2 PETER

Helping Christians to know Jesus better

INTRODUCTION

- The apostles Peter and Paul died in the city of Rome around the year 65. Peter wrote this letter to Christians shortly before he died. He cared a lot about the people he wrote to. He wanted to make sure they didn't get wrong ideas that would take them away from Jesus. He started and ended the letter with words about knowing Jesus more. Everything in between follows that same theme.

- Peter probably wrote this letter some time between A.D. 64 and 67.

OVERVIEW

1. "From Peter (an *apostle* and servant of Jesus Christ) to Christians everywhere. I hope you will be full of *grace* and peace through knowing God the Father and Jesus our Lord."

2. "God's power gave us everything we need to be saved from our sin and obey God. Because he gave us everything, we should behave how God wants us to behave. This shows that we have really been saved from our sins and are really sorry for them, and not just talking about it to sound Christian."

3. "Remember: we didn't make things up about Jesus. I was there and I saw and heard the things that happened, including when God the Father said about Jesus, *'This is my son, whom I love.'*[167] I wrote to you before and I am writing to you again to try and help you think about things in the right way. Remember the free gift of forgiveness and how God wants us to obey him."

4. "Lots of people will say that Jesus is never coming again, but God already planned for when it will happen. When it does, *The [skies] will disappear with a roar,* and everything *will be destroyed by fire.*[168] It hasn't happened yet because God is patient, *not wanting anyone to perish, but everyone to come to repentance,*[169] but one day the world will end and Jesus will come suddenly. We can look forward to it because that is when we will be with God properly. Looking forward to what God will do for us should make us want to obey him even more. Paul the *apostle* writes about this as well and what he writes is also part of the Bible."

5. "Some people will tell lies about Jesus. They'll say he is not really God, or that God doesn't mind if you *sin*. They do all the sins they want to do and don't really care

---

167. 2 Peter 1:17.
168. 2 Peter 3:10.
169. 2 Peter 3:9.

about others. God will punish them for all that. Do not believe them. Instead, get to know Jesus better and better."

LEARNING FROM 2 PETER

1. If we are Christians, God lives in us and we can look forward to being with him forever. He has given us everything we need to help us want to love God, and to actually love him in the way we live. (See overview paragraph 2).

   Bible references: 2 Chronicles 20:17; 2 Timothy 2:21.
   Questions: Can you think of times when you don't want to obey God? What or who can help you when you feel like that?

2. Be careful of false teachings about Jesus. Don't just trust what people say – first check what the Bible says, because the Bible is God's Word (See overview paragraphs 3 and 5).

   Bible references: 2 Peter 2:1, 3; Psalm 119:86a; 2 Corinthians 10:5.
   Questions: Where do we go to find the truth about Jesus?

3. Jesus will come again and when he does, all those who reject God will be punished. Those who have had their sins forgiven will go to be with God in *heaven* forever. It will be a wonderful and terrible day (See overview paragraph 4).

   Bible references: 2 Peter 3:8-10; Malachi 4:5-6; Romans 2:9-10.
   Question: How do you feel about the day of God, when Jesus will come again?

SALVATION THREAD

"[the day of God] will bring about the destruction of the heavens by fire, and the elements will melt in the heat. But in keeping with his promise we are looking forward to a new *heaven* and a new earth, the home of righteousness" (2 Peter 3:12-13).

The Judgment will be a time of massive and awesome destruction, but for God's people it will be the best day of their lives, when Jesus welcomes his people into his home to be with him forever. 2 Peter is one of the last books of the New Testament to be written and it encourages Christians to look forward to the day when Jesus comes again. All *sin*, death, pain and sadness will be put away forever by God, who will bring life and happiness to all his people.

When he wrote this letter, Peter wanted people to understand that if they really believed their sins were forgiven and that Jesus was coming again, they would live for Jesus. Like then, God's people today look forward to when Jesus will come again, and use the opportunity of life on earth to keep serving him until then.

Key Verse: "But grow in the *grace* and knowledge of our Lord and Savior Jesus Christ. To him be *glory* both now and for ever! Amen." (2 Peter 3:18).

The books of
1, 2 & 3 JOHN

WELCOME

1 JOHN

Living in love through Jesus

INTRODUCTION

- By the time John wrote this, most of his fellow *disciples* were dead for nearly thirty years, and it was about sixty years since Jesus went back to heaven. In that time some people had started telling lies about Jesus, saying that he was never really a man, and that people could behave any way they wanted. John knew this was a dangerous teaching that would take people away from God, and eternal life, so he wrote this letter.

- John probably wrote this letter some time between A.D. 67 and 100.

OVERVIEW

1. "Jesus has always been alive. We knew him when he was on earth and we tell you about him now so that you can have a relationship with him and God the Father."

2. "God is completely good. If we say we love God but want to keep doing what is wrong all the time, we are lying and do not really love God."

3. "However, we are not perfect– we need to admit to God we are wrong and then he will clean us from our *sin*. Jesus' death pays the price for our *sin* and the *sin* of everyone else who asks God to forgive them."

4. "Obeying God's commands and loving other Christians shows that we love God."

5. "Many people have gone away from the church because they did not believe that Jesus is God. It is important that you remember Jesus is God. It is because of Jesus that we can live forever with God. Isn't it amazing that God has done that for us – he even calls us his children! He is perfect and if we are really with him we will not want to do what is wrong. Also, people who love God, love other Christians."

6. "Really loving each other means taking care of each other and being kind; living that way helps us to know that we belong to God. All love comes from God and sending Jesus to die for us showed us that love."

7. "Be careful when people say things to you about God. Make sure that they believe Jesus came to earth as a man and that he is also God, before you believe what they say about him. God himself tells us about Jesus, and if we don't believe God it is like saying he is a liar."

8. *"We know also that the Son of God has come and has given us understanding, so that we may know him who is true. And we are in him who is true – even in his Son Jesus Christ. He is the true God and eternal life. Dear children, keep yourselves from idols."*[170]

---

170. 1 John 5:20-21.

LEARNING FROM 1 JOHN

1. Jesus is God and came to earth as a man. If we don't believe that, then we don't know God (See overview paragraphs 1, 5–8).

    Bible references: 1 John 2:22; 5:1, 12; 2 Timothy 2:21; Hebrews 1:3, 6.

    Questions: Who do you believe that Jesus is?

2. If we love Jesus, then we will obey God and when we *sin*, God will forgive us (See overview paragraphs 2–4).

    Bible references: 1 John 1:8-9; Joshua 22:5; Romans 6:2, 11.

    Question: If Jesus died so that our sins can be taken away, how does that make you feel about your *sin*?

3. Because of what Jesus has done for us, and the love that God has shown us, we should love God and other people (See overview paragraphs 2 and 4–6).

    Bible references: 1 John 4:11-12, 19, 21; John 15:12.

    Questions: How has God loved us? How can you show that you love God and that you love other people? (see 1 John 3:18).

SALVATION THREAD

When people try to be religious, they hope that if they do lots of good things God will do nice things for them or let them into heaven. They can never be sure of being saved because they never know whether they have done enough. But that's not how it is with Jesus.

John wrote this letter to help people be sure they have been forgiven by God and saved from sin, instead of just hoping that maybe they are forgiven. His letter says, "I write these things to you who believe in the name of the Son of God so that you may know that you have eternal life" (1 John 5:13).

To help Christians know that they are forgiven, John gave some signs to look out for:

"We know that we have come to know him if we obey his commands" (2:3).

"Dear children, let us not love with words or tongue but with actions and in truth. This then is how we know that we belong to the truth, and how we set our hearts at rest in his presence whenever our hearts condemn us" (3:18-19).

"And this is how we know that he lives in us: We know it by the Spirit he gave us" (3:24).

"If anyone acknowledges that Jesus is the Son of God, God lives in him and he in God … In this way, love is made complete among us so that we will have confidence on the day of judgment … There is no fear in love" (4:15–18).

"Everyone who believes that Jesus is the Christ is born of God …" (5:1).

Key Verse: "… this is his command: to believe in the name of his Son, Jesus Christ, and to love one another …" (1 John 3:23).

2 & 3 JOHN

Love one another

INTRODUCTION

- If you visited a town to tell people about Jesus, you would expect the church to welcome you - right? However, John had a problem: someone from a church he knew was trying to keep *Christians* away! But John also wanted people to be careful about welcoming people into the church – if they spread lies about Jesus (which would be very dangerous), they should not be made welcome. In everything, John's main concern was that people would love each other.

- John probably wrote these letters some time between A.D. 85 and 95.

OVERVIEW

1. "To the chosen lady and her children, whom I love in the truth. *It has given me great joy to find some of your children walking in the truth, just as the Father commanded us.*[171] And now I give you an old command: love one another."

2. "Many liars, who say that Jesus never came as a man, are going around spreading their lies. Watch out that you don't fall into their trap. To stay with God you must keep to Jesus' teaching. If any of these liars come to your house, don't welcome them in because to do that is helping their evil work."

3. "I have a lot to write to you but I would rather come and see you."

4. "*To my dear friend Gaius, whom I love in the truth.*[172] I pray that all would go well with your body and soul."

5. "It gave me great joy to hear of your faithfulness to the truth. Hearing that my children are walking in the truth is my greatest joy. You are faithful in helping the *Christian* workers who come to your town, even though you don't know them. They are working for Jesus' sake and in helping them we are working together with them for the truth."

6. "I wrote to the church but Diotrephes, who thinks he's really important, won't have anything to do with us and spreads lies about us. He also refuses to welcome Christian workers from other towns, and if anyone else welcomes them, he puts those people out of the church. That is evil behavior. Copy good, not evil. Those who do good are from God, but those who do evil are not from God."

---

171. 2 John 4.
172. 3 John 1.

250

7. "Hopefully I'll see you soon. *Peace to you. The friends here send their greetings. Greet the friends there by name.*"[173]

LEARNING FROM 2 & 3 JOHN

1. John loved the people he was writing to because they loved the truth; they loved Jesus. If we love Jesus we will love other people who love Jesus (See overview paragraphs 2, 4–6).

   Bible references: 2 John 1-2, 3 John 13-14; Colossians 4:7.

   Questions: What makes you love or like people? Why do you like to be with them?

2. If we are Christians, then seeing other people become Christians and follow Jesus will be a big thing we want, and will bring us true happiness (See overview paragraphs 2 and 4–5).

   Bible references: 2 John 4; 3 John 3-4; Luke 15:7; Romans 9:3.

   Questions: If you really want something, or you know that something will make you really happy, what would you do to get it? How much do you want other people to know about Jesus?

3. Some people in John's time, who wanted to act in a loving way, welcomed anyone into their home, even if some of those people were going round spreading lies about Jesus. We should remember that the truth is important and we must help people to know the truth about Jesus, so that they can know Jesus himself (See overview paragraphs 2 and 6). So be kind to everyone, but don't help people to spread lies.

   Bible references: 3 John 10-11; Psalm 26:3; 1 Corinthians 8:2-3.

   Question: If you heard someone telling lies about Jesus, what would you do? Sometimes the best thing might be to walk away, sometimes it's best to say what you believe about Jesus. What do you think would happen if you told your friends what you believe about Jesus? Have you asked God to help you?

SALVATION THREAD

Jesus is life and truth and love, and John helps us to understand all those things come together – you can't split them apart.

If you truly love Jesus because you know and believe the truth about him, if you have repented and you trust in God, then you have life with him and from him.

Love without truth is useless. Truth without love is lifeless. Life without love is meaningless. Truth without life is loveless.

"I am the way, the truth and the life. No-one comes to the Father except through me ...Whoever has my commands and obeys them, he is the one who loves me. He who loves me will be loved by my Father, and I too will love him and show myself to him" (John 14:6, 21).

Key Verse: "*Grace, mercy and peace from God the Father and from Jesus Christ, the Father's Son, will be with us in truth and love*" (2 John 3).

---

173. 3 John 14.

The book of
JUDE

JUDE

Finding faith and truth in a faithless world

INTRODUCTION

- The best things in life are what the *devil* and bad people attack the most. So, even though Jude wanted to celebrate God's *grace* with the Christians, he also had to warn them that it was important to defend the truth. He was really concerned about them! There were several people called Jude in the Bible, and this one was probably the brother of Jesus.

- Jude probably wrote his letter some time between A.D. 64 and 66.

OVERVIEW

1. "From Jude, *to those who have been called, who are loved by God the Father and kept by Jesus Christ.*[174] May you have much mercy, peace and love."

2. "Dear friends, I was really keen to write to you about the *salvation* we share, but then I felt I needed to write instead to urge you to defend the *faith* – the truth about God that has been given to you. Some people who don't know God have mixed in with God's people and are lying about Jesus and teaching wrong things. They say it's okay to live how you want and disobey God. I need to remind you that it's most important to believe what is right, and to obey God."

3. "Those false teachers are rude about things they don't understand. They are selfish, greedy and full of hate, spoiling your church. God will punish them. Remember, the apostles of Jesus told us that there would be people like this, who laugh at the truth and do what they want. They do not have the Holy Spirit in them, and they cause division in the church."

4. "But you, dear friends, grow stronger in your *faith*, pray with the wisdom of the Holy Spirit. Stay in God's love until the great *mercy* of Jesus comes again to bring you to eternal life."

5. "*Be merciful to those who doubt; snatch others from the fire*[175] of death by helping them understand the truth. But be careful that the lies about God's truth don't burn you – they will take you away from God."

6. "To God, *who is able to keep you from falling and to present you before his glorious presence without fault and with great joy – to the only God our Savior be glory, majesty, power and authority, through Jesus Christ our Lord, before all ages, now and for evermore. Amen.*"[176]

---

174 Jude verse 1.
175. Jude verses 22-23.
176. Jude verses 24-25.

LEARNING FROM JUDE

1. God says we must obey him; having our sins forgiven doesn't mean it's okay to be sinful (See overview paragraphs 2–3).

   Bible references: Jude 3–16; Isaiah 44:22; Romans 6:11-12.

   Questions: If someone said they may do whatever they like because their sins are forgiven, what would you tell them?

2. When people don't know about God or have the wrong idea about God, we should be kind to them and try to help them by showing them the truth about what God says. Jude told people to "be merciful" to those who don't understand (See overview paragraph 5).

   Bible references: Jude 2, 22-23; Deuteronomy 4:30-31; Galatians 6:1.

   Questions: What did Jude want people to have? Look at the beginning of his letter. What do you think about people when they don't understand something that you think is easy? Do you sometimes just think they're silly, or do you try to help them?

3. Satan's lies are designed to divide God's people and take people away from God. We cannot resist those lies on our own so we should ask God to help us (See overview paragraphs 1, 3, 5–6).

   Bible references: Jude 1-2, 24-25; Proverbs 4:13; Jeremiah 23:30-32; Ephesians 6:11-12.

   Questions: Have you ever been friends with someone, other people said bad things about them, and soon everyone is saying those nasty things? Or maybe that's happened to you? Often people will believe things just because other people say them.

SALVATION THREAD

Jude wrote about one of the big church problems from the years after Jesus went back to heaven. It was the wrong idea that being a *Christian* is just about saying the right words and WHAM! ... magically you're saved from your sins.

People who say that, don't understand what happens when someone becomes a *Christian*. Paul the *apostle* explained it like this: "... if anyone is in Christ, he is a new creation; the old has gone, the new has come! All this is from God, who *reconciled* us to himself in Christ ..."[177] So we haven't just been given a badge that says we belong to a different club, and we haven't just been given a ticket that says we can go to *heaven* when we die. No, we have been made new again! That's why we sometimes call it being "born again."[178] Jesus died to take away our *sin*. God makes us new again so that we can love him ... so if we are truly saved by God we will want to obey him. If we don't want to obey God, we are not truly saved by him. That's why Jude was so concerned that people understand the difference between truth and lies about Jesus.

Key Verse: "Keep yourselves in God's love as you wait for the *mercy* of our Lord Jesus Christ to bring you to eternal life" (Jude 21).

---

177. 2 Corinthians 5:17-18.
178. John 3:3-7.

The book of
REVELATION

REVELATION

Everything is made perfect again, forever

INTRODUCTION

- Because John told people about Jesus, the rulers did not like him. They thought he was causing trouble and they wanted to get him away from their town. They sent him to an island called Patmos and forced him to stay there. He wrote this book from Patmos, and sent it to seven churches in the country we now call Turkey.

- The start of the Bible tells how God made everything perfect, but people spoiled it. The end of the Bible tells us how God will make everything perfect again, forever. It tells us what will happen when the world ends.

- John wrote this revelation from God around A.D. 95/96.

OVERVIEW

1. "This revelation went from God the Father to Jesus, God's Son. Then an angel told it to John."

2. "I was awake and the angel showed me an amazing vision of Jesus, who had a message for seven churches. Some of them were in much trouble. People were horrible to them for being Christians, but Jesus encouraged them to keep following him. Some of the churches were not doing as well as they thought they were, and others thought that being a *Christian* meant you could do what you wanted. Jesus told them to be sorry, and promised wonderful things in *heaven* for people who followed him."

3. "Then I saw *heaven*, and God being worshiped. Jesus, because he died to save people from their sins, was the only one good enough to open a scroll with a special message. It told about very bad things that would happen, but it also said God's people would be kept safe."

4. "Then angels played their trumpets and horrible things happened like the sun went dark and lots of people were killed by bad angels. But even though God was using these bad things that happened to show people how serious sin is, they were still not sorry for all the wrong things they were doing."

5. "There was a battle later with *Satan* and his angels who were beaten by the angel Michael and lots of other angels from God. *Satan* then went off to try and hurt Christians, and to trick other people into thinking he was God."

6. "Then God defeated *Satan* in a huge battle and threw *Satan* into hell for ever. People who rejected God were also punished, including those who were very nasty to Christians."

7. "God then makes a wonderful new place to live with him, so that everyone who accepted his free gift of forgiveness can be with him forever."

LEARNING FROM REVELATION

1. There are only two kinds of people: those who reject God and those who have accepted him. They will be divided forever on judgment day. Those who accepted God go to be with him forever in *heaven*. Those who rejected him go to be without him in forever, in *hell* (See overview paragraphs 2–4, 6–7).

    Bible references: Revelation 20:15, 21:1-8; Psalm 37:28; Matthew 25:32-33.

    Question: To accept God includes believing what he says. What are some of the important things that God said in the Bible about Jesus? About sin? About forgiveness? About God's love for us?

2. *Satan* was defeated when Jesus died and rose again. At the end of the world God will defeat him again, forever. We can praise God that however bad things seem to be he will make everything perfect again in the end (See overview paragraphs 3, 5–7).

    Bible references: Revelation 20:10, 21:1-2; 1 Corinthians 15:55; 2 Peter 3:13.

    Questions: What are some of the bad things that happen in the world? What will it be like for Christians to live in a perfect place forever with God?

3. Jesus looks after Christians, even when they are having a bad time. This sometimes means telling them what they are doing right, and what they are doing wrong, to help them love him more. Other times it might be just reminding them that he is always with them, as he promised (See overview paragraph 2).

    Bible references: Revelation 2 and 3; Matthew 28:20.

    Questions: What were the churches doing wrong? How did Jesus encourage them? How do you love God in your life?

SALVATION THREAD

The Bible is about God: what he does to bring glory to his name and save his people. John's big revelation from God about the end of the world started in chapter 4 with a picture of God's throne in heaven, and ended with the second coming of Jesus in chapter 22.

Christians can take comfort from Revelation. It has a *prophecy* about the ultimate defeat of *Satan* that began when Jesus rose from the dead. God has the victory, and just as Jesus rose from the dead, God's people will rise to be with him forever.

"Now the dwelling of God is with men, and he will live with them. They will be his people, and God himself will be with them and be their God. He will wipe every tear from their eyes. There will be no more death or mourning or crying or pain, for the old order of things has passed away."[179] What an amazing promise God made, and still makes to all those who turn to him for forgiveness. Are you looking forward to that day?

Key Verse: "To him who sits on the throne and to the Lamb be praise and honor and glory and power, for ever and ever!" (Revelation 5:13).

---

179. Revelation 21:3-4.

KEY WORDS

Apostle: Someone who saw Jesus while he was on earth. God gave them a special job to do miracles and preach about Jesus. The *disciples* and Paul are examples of apostles (Romans 1:1; 1 Peter 1:1).

Christian: Someone who trusts God for the forgiveness of their sins through the death of the Lord Jesus Christ on the *cross*, and shows they love God through how they live (Acts 11:26; 26:28).

Circumcision: God first told Abraham to do this, and then said that all Jewish males needed to do it, to show that they were set apart for God. It meant cutting off the outer piece of skin from the end of a boy's penis when he reached eight days old. It hurt for a little while but soon healed. We don't do that nowadays (in the time of the New *Covenant*). When we become Christians, the sign that we are set apart for God is when we are baptized (Genesis 17; Matthew 28:19).

Covenant: A covenant in the Bible is an agreement between God and his people. The Old Covenant lasted until Jesus died on the cross, and since then we have been in the time of the New Covenant (Jeremiah 31:31-33; Luke 22:20).

Cross (also crucifixion): Jesus was killed on a cross. To kill someone on a cross was called a crucifixion. The *Romans* nailed Jesus to two pieces of wood that they made into a cross while it was lying on the ground. Then they lifted up the cross and put the bottom of it into a hole in the ground, so that it stood up. They left the person hanging there until they died, which usually took a couple of days (John 19:17; 1 Corinthians 1:17).

Devil: Another name for Satan: the enemy of God and all people. Jesus described him as the "father of lies" (Matthew 13:37–39; John 8:44).

Disciples: When we think of the disciples we usually think of the twelve men who spent a lot of time with Jesus. They were not the only people who followed Jesus while he was on earth but they were the ones Jesus chose to be with him the most. The word "Disciple" means follower. Christians are also disciples of Jesus. The twelve disciples were: Peter, James, John, Andrew, Philip, Bartholomew, Matthew, Thomas, James (son of Alphaeus), Thaddaeus, Simon and Judas Iscariot. Matthias replaced Judas as one of the twelve disciples (Matthew 28:19; Mark 3:13-19; Acts 1:12-26).

Exile: To be taken away, or sent away from your country by force. In the Bible, the most famous *exile* was when Judah was defeated by the Babylonian armies. After defeat, many of the Jews were taken away to Babylon where they stayed for seventy years. Before that, the northern tribes of Israel were defeated, and taken into *exile* by the Assyrians. (2 Kings 17:21-23; 2 Chronicles 36:15-25)

Faith: To believe in something that you cannot see with your eyes. To have faith in God is to believe in him and what he says, especially the *gospel*. If we have faith in God, we want to live for him (Isaiah 26:2; Hebrews 11:1, 6).

Gentile: A Gentile is someone who is not a Jew, and a Jew is someone who belongs to the country of Israel. So, most people in the world are Gentiles as most of us don't come from Israel. God's people in the time of the Old *Covenant* were mainly people from Israel. Now, God's people come from all over the world (Romans 1:16-17; Ephesians 3:6).

Grace: God's attitude of love to people, which they do not deserve. When God fills people with his grace, it means that they receive blessings they do not deserve. It also refers to having that same attitude of grace that God does. All Christians should show God's grace to other people (John 1:17; Acts 15:11).

Glory: God's glory is his perfection, sinlessness, wisdom, knowledge of everything, love, holiness, awesomeness, greatness, bigness and total power … all rolled into one. Christians are called to show those things about God in the way that they live, and to "give glory to God". This means for example that when something great happens we thank God for it, rather than acting like it was an accident or that we should get all the credit ourselves (Isaiah 42:12; Revelation 19:7).

Gospel: The word gospel means 'good news'. Christians disagree about many things, but they agree on the gospel, which cannot be changed. It is the gift of eternal life with forgiveness of sins from God, which we receive after we *repent*. 'Gospel' is also used to refer to the Bible books written by Matthew, Mark, Luke and John (John 3:16-18; Galatians 1:6-7).

Heaven: Heaven is a real place. It is where Christians go when they die, to be with God forever. It is a more wonderful place than you can ever imagine (Exodus 20:22; Matthew 18:10).

Hell: Hell is a real place. It is where people go when they die, if they have not had their sins forgiven. It is away from God and is a more horrible place than you can ever imagine (Matthew 25:46; 2 Peter 2:4).

High priest: The highest-ranking priest. He had the special job of going into the Holy of Holies in the *temple* once every year to offer a special *sacrifice* for the *Israelites*. Jesus is described as the High priest (Hebrews 4:14; 9:25-26; 13:11-12).

Holy: This means "set apart". God's people are "set apart" from sin for God, and must live a "set apart" life, which means to be obedient to God's commands. God is the ultimate example of what it means to be holy: He is right and good in everything and always does what is best (Leviticus 20:26; 1 Peter 1:16).

Israelites (also Jews): People of the nation of Israel (Exodus 1:1-7; Romans 10:1).

Justification; Justified: When God makes us 'right' with him. We are born going against God, but if we repent and our sins are forgiven, God has made us 'right' with him. It is as though we were in court for a crime and the judge said, "Not guilty" (Acts 13:39; Romans 4:25–5:1).

Law: The first five books of the Bible, also known as the 'Pentateuch' or 'Torah'. When Jews referred to the Law they meant those five books, and all that is in them about what God said they must and must not do. The Law is there not because we can get to *heaven* if we obey it enough. It is there to show us see we can't obey it, so that we turn to Jesus to forgive us, and trust in him (Joshua 1:8; Philippians 3:9).

Mercy: When someone deserves to be punished but they are not punished, it is because they have been shown "mercy". We deserve nothing but punishment from God because we were against him the whole time since we were children, but if he has forgiven our sins that means he has shown us "mercy" (Nehemiah 9:31; Ephesians 2:4-5).

Messiah: The holy one from God promised throughout the Old Testament, who would save his people. Most of the Jews misunderstood this to mean that God was going to send someone who would save them from the people who had invaded their country. What God really meant was that he would send his Son to save his people from their sins (Hosea 1:7; John 4:25-26).

Persecution (persecute, persecuted): Being treated badly because of *faith* in God. It can just be when someone says horrible things to a Christian. But throughout history – even today - persecution can mean Christians are kicked out of their job, or put in prison just for telling people about Jesus, or refusing to worship a false god. Sometimes Christians are beaten up or even killed (Matthew 5:11-12; Hebrews 10:33).

Pharisee; Pharisees: Jewish religious leaders. They were very strict about the *law*, and made up a lot of their own laws on top of God's laws. It discouraged many people because God seemed so hard to please, which made them feel far away from God. Pharisees made people think they had to be good enough for God, instead of trusting God to forgive their sins. They were some of the people who plotted to get Jesus killed (Matthew 12:14; 23:13).

Philistines: Enemies of God's people the *Israelites* during the time of the Old Testament. They worshiped false gods (Judges 13:1; 16:23).

Pride: Thinking that you are better than other people, or better than you really are (Proverbs 16:18: Romans 12:3).

Priest: Priests worked in the *temple* during Old *Covenant* times, looking after the *temple* and offering sacrifices for the people. Since Jesus died, we no longer need anyone to make sacrifices for us, because Jesus is the ultimate *sacrifice* (See also *High priest*) (Exodus 29:44; Ezekiel 40:45).

Promised land: When God rescued the *Israelites* from slavery in Egypt, after forty years in the desert they went into the country of Canaan – the "Promised land". God had promised he would take them to that wonderful country, and that He would bless them as long as they stayed obedient to him. Christians now look forward to a different and better Promised land: *heaven* (Deuteronomy 26:8-9; Hebrews 11:16).

Prophet (see also prophecy): Someone who was given an exact message from God to pass on to God's people. Sometimes this meant telling people what was about to happen or what they needed to do. It would often also give a picture of what would happen much later, such as when Jesus came to earth, or at the end of the world. A prophecy is one of those messages (2 Kings 3:11; Acts 7:52-53).

Reconcile; Reconciles; Reconciled: To reconcile is to bring back a friendly relationship between two people or two sets of people, where that relationship has gone bad. The Bible talks about our need to be reconciled to God – our *sin* puts us in a bad relationship with God and it is only through Jesus that we can be reconciled with God (Acts 7:26; Romans 5:10).

Repent: To know that you are a sinner and that you can't do anything about it on your own; to ask God to forgive you and take that *sin* away by forgiving you. And to turn from your *sin* towards obeying God. A *Christian* is someone who has repented (1 Kings 8:47-50; Matthew 4:17).

Righteous/Righteousness: To behave in a righteous way is to do what is right based on God's Word, even when others are against us. When God gives righteousness to his people it means that Jesus' perfect obedience is given to them. Because of this, on Judgement Day God will judge his people based not on their sinful nature but based on Jesus' righteousness (Psalm 119:137; Romans 3:10, 21-22).

Romans: People from Rome, in Italy, called Romans, took over all of Italy. After that, they invaded and took over other countries, like Israel. When they invaded Israel they killed many people, and worshiped false gods, and made the Jews pay them lots of money. So, the Jews hated them (Luke 2:1; John 11:48).

Sacrifice: *Sin* is so serious that it can only be paid for by death. Before Jesus came to die on the *cross*, God told his people to kill animals as a sign that they were asking God to forgive them for their sins, and that one day Jesus' death would pay for them (Romans 6:23; 7:25).

Salvation: What God does for creation, and especially people, saving them from the power of *sin* through the work of Jesus (Romans 8:20-21; 1 Peter 1:9).

Satan: Another name for the *devil*, it means 'the accuser'. Satan accuses God's people, even though their sins are forgiven, and tries to make them feel bad. He wants them to either they think they are not forgiven after all, or for them to try and prove to God they are good enough. Christians should remember that God has defeated Satan, and he will go to his eternal punishment when Jesus comes again (Romans 16:20; Revelation 12:9-10).

Sin: Sin is what is in us and what we do. Because Adam and Eve disobeyed God, all of us are born with a sinful nature. This means that what comes naturally to us is what we want, not what God wants (Psalm 51:5; Matthew 5:29).

Temple: This was like a church – it was where the Jews worshiped God. King Solomon built the first one according to a design and measurements given to his father King David, by God. In the New *Covenant*, the temple is used to mean every Christians in the world. Using that word shows that the whole life of Christians should honor God and give worship to him through obedience and love (1 Chronicles 28:11-12; 1 Corinthians 3:16).

Ten Commandments: These are ten rules for how to live, given by God to Moses when Moses went up a mountain called Sinai, while the *Israelites* were in the desert after escaping from Egypt (Exodus 20:1-17; Romans 13:9). Jesus talked about them 1,500 years later, showing that they were still as important as before.

Tribes of Israel: The twelve people groups that made up the country of Israel, named after sons of Jacob: Judah, Reuben, Gad, Asher, Napthali, Manasseh, Simeon, Levi, Issacher, Zebulun, Joseph, and Benjamin. When the *Israelites* came out of Egypt and went into the promised land, each of the tribes was given a portion of land, except the tribe of Levi, who were given parts of all the other tribes' areas. Also, there was no tribe in the Old Testament named after Jacob's son Joseph. Instead they had two tribes named after his sons: Ephraim and Manasseh. (Ezekiel 48 and Revelation 7:4-8).